52

OF·THE

BEST TOYS
AND
GAMES FOR
YOUR CHILD

Phil Phillips

OLIVER
NELSON

THOMAS NELSON PUBLISHERS
Nashville

To
A highly qualified and well-deserving review
panel, my children . . .
Taylor, Hayes, and Corbin

And to special friends
Roddy and Denise Qualls
and their daughters Sonja and Jennifer,
whose generous and faithful support through the years
has helped make work possible

Published in Nashville, Tennessee, by Oliver-Nelson Books, a division of Thomas Nelson, Inc., Publishers, and distributed in Canada by Lawson Falle, Ltd., Cambridge, Ontario.

Printed in the United States of America.

Library of Congress Cataloging-in-Publication Data

Phillips, Phil.
    52 of the best toys and games for your child / Phil Phillips.
        p.   cm.
    ISBN 0-8407-9639-0
    1. Toys. 2. Games. I. Title. II. Title: Fifty-two of the best toys and games for your child.
GV1218.5.P47   1992
790.1'922—dc20   92-15372
                                                           CIP

1 2 3 4 5 6 — 97 96 95 94 93 92

♦ Contents

♦ Introduction

I often say, "We grown-ups get up and go to work in the morning. Children get up and go to play." An average child will spend some fifteen thousand hours in play before the age of seven. Play is, in a very real way, a child's work.

Play is the means by which a child explores the world, learning what works and what doesn't, which roles are comfortable, and which behaviors are rewarding and rewarded. Play enhances a child's physical development—providing opportunities for acquisition of motor skills, perception skills, and discrimination skills—and social and intellectual development. Play is active; it takes effort, calling on all senses and physical facilities.

Toys and games are the tools of play. They are the props that give impetus to a child's imagination. Children play with toys and games to "try on" life.

Last year, more than nine hundred companies across the United States produced nearly 150 million toys. Many won't reappear next year. (In some cases, fine toys will fall by the wayside for lack of promotion and exposure in the marketplace.) Others are forty-year standards. All in all, the multibillion-dollar toy industry is highly competitive. The commercials, advertisements, and in-store displays propelling this industry can make one's head swim with confusion.

How do you determine which toys have maximum benefit for your child? These are the ten guidelines used in defining a *good toy* for inclusion in this book.

1. A good toy promotes a constructive expression of feelings, thoughts, and ideas It promotes individual creativity, learning, and positive socialization. I do *not* recommend war toys in this volume; neither do I recommend toys based on children's television programs that have an extremely high number of violent incidents per episode.

2. A good toy calls upon a child's imagination and encourages imaginative play "scripted" by the child Numerous toys currently on the market are based on children's movies and cartoon serials. I do *not* recommend them. They promote what I call preprogrammed play. As the result of watching a television program featuring certain characters, a child derives an understanding of how a character is supposed to act, move, or talk. In playing with an action figure based on such a program, a child inevitably gives to that toy the characteristics previously portrayed. He becomes a "mimic" of a prior characterization, not the creator of one.

3. A good toy is durable   I recommend toys that can be washed, cleaned, repaired, and reused year after year. Ask yourself, Will the toy last longer than the box it comes in? If you suspect it won't, don't buy it.

4. A good toy is challenging and stimulating, without going beyond the child's skill or maturity level   Most toys provide a recommended age range as part of the packaging. A parent should always pay attention to those guidelines. They are derived by manufacturers after months of testing with children. You will know where your child falls within the recommended range and how your child's skill levels compare to those of other children of the same age. Thus, you will be able to calculate how many years your child may have to play with the toy.

Age five is something of a watershed age in toy manufacturing. Children five years and under should not be allowed to play with toys that have small items, stuffing, liquids, or appendages that might be swallowed or inhaled and cause choking or suffocation.

5. A good toy is child-powered   Very few toys recommended in this book require batteries or electrical power. If a non-battery-powered toy is available next to one with batteries, opt for the one that your child must manipulate and power. A child-powered toy requires a child to engage physically and mentally—and, thus, creatively—with the toy. Battery-powered toys require a child to watch.

Furthermore, batteries pose a potential toxicity and choking hazard for young children.

6. A good toy has long-lasting "play value" A toy should compel a child's interest and interaction for years, not minutes. Many toys on the market are "play specific." They have one use, one action, one role. Choose toys that can be used in multiple ways for different looks, designs, or results. Games should hold a child's interest for repeated visits, not be boring after one run-through or after the initial conquest.

7. A good toy is a safe toy Always look for small parts, sharp edges, projectiles, and potential dangers should the toy break. Cloth toys should be treated for flame resistance. Painted toys should be painted with nontoxic paints.

A good toy should not require constant supervision to ensure safety or correct use by a child for which it is age-appropriate.

Don't buy a toy without looking at it. Many people purchase toys based on the box or packaging. Open the box and evaluate the contents for yourself.

8. A good toy results in happy dreams and a healthy soul I do *not* recommend toys that promote occult behaviors (such as crystal balls, Ouija boards, magic wands, and so forth). I do *not* recommend toys rooted in fear or repulsion—such as monsters, ghouls, ghosts, goblins, or "gross" fantasy creatures. I am a strong advocate of toys that protect innocence.

9. A good toy engages a child creatively as an active participant   For the most part, this book does not address computers, computer games, video games, and other electronic games. Many video games and electronic toys require reflex actions more than logic or creativity.

10. A good toy is shared or promotes group interaction   Many toys are geared toward the "alone child." Whenever possible, choose toys that invite children to play together, communicate with one another, and share experiences, ideas, and decision-making and problem-solving skills.

In buying toys, adults should always ask themselves this overriding question: What is my child going to do with this toy? Begin your appraisal of a toy or game with your child, not with the toy.

Finally, bear in mind these critical points:

- *No child is qualified to choose toys.* Children are influenced by advertising, packaging, cartoons, and peer pressure. Children's whims are transient. What they want today, they may not want tomorrow. It is always the adult's responsibility to choose what the adult perceives to be the wisest choice of toy. A toy should be purchased not as a symbol of social status but as a learning tool.
- *A child does not need lots of toys.* Children do not suffer psychological damage from not get-

ting a toy. Don't give in to whining or pleading. A toy is a gift . . . a reward . . . a good thing worth waiting for . . . a treat . . . and above all, a learning and development tool. Rotate your child's toys.

* *You are your child's best toy.* If given a choice between playing with a thing and playing with a loving, nurturing adult, the child will nearly always choose the adult! Part of your role as a parent or loving adult is to nurture a child in play and to teach a child how to play.

Do what you can to promote your child's creativity and curiosity. Sit down on the floor and play along for a few minutes. Get the plot or the play action started. Encourage make-believe roles. Your child will benefit from your involvement, and you'll enjoy those moments for years to come as precious memories.

The toys and games in this book should be regarded as suggestions of "type." Similar items are frequently manufactured or distributed by more than one company. To the best of our knowledge, the items mentioned are available at the time of publication. We cannot, however, guarantee the availability of the items.

1 ♦ Stimulation Toys for Infants

For centuries, adults held a widespread belief that infants don't really "do" anything. Ah, but they do! They explore! From the minute a child is born, he actively responds to his environment. Literally thrust into a brand-new world, the infant begins immediately to attempt to make sense of it. Toys for infants should help them develop in the following ways.

Develop the Sense of Touch Expose your infant to different fabrics and surfaces. Encourage her to "touch" and "feel" with **Feel & Match Textures** (Lauri). Touch the various materials—including felt, plastic, rubber, and cork—to your child's face, hands, arms, legs, and feet. As your child grows and is able to play with the toy alone, she will develop the ability to touch softly and understand more about how to handle fragile objects.

Develop the Ability to Differentiate Sounds Rattles have been a baby's mainstay for centuries (ever since the first gourd was used as a rattle). Provide a variety of shapes and sounds. Make sure all are safe for your baby to chew on;

they should have no protrusions under 1.25 inches in diameter and should be crackproof. Squeaker toys should not have noise mechanisms that might snap out and become lodged in your baby's throat. Avoid, however, exposing your infant to toys that emit loud sounds or loud music. They are frightening and can damage the ear.

Look for the **Twin Rattle** (Ambi) with its smiling faces. The **Spin-a-Sound** (Johnson & Johnson) "dumbbell" has bright primary-colored paddles, which produce a variety of sounds, and the toy also has a crank and dial. **Spinning Rattle** (T. C. Timber) can be used as a top, rattle, or teether. Gund makes a **Half-Pint Milk Bottle** in pink or blue that is a soft squeezable squeaker toy. **Flatjack Rabbit** (North American Bear Company) is a bunny-shaped rattle in blue or pink garb.

Focus and Coordinate Eye Movements

Expose your infant to bright colors. The **Crib Activity Arch** (Johnson & Johnson) is a combination infant gym and mobile. Soft toys are suspended from a patterned arch, providing stimulation of moving colors and objects. The arch is flexible and gives when tugged so your baby will be unable to use it to hoist himself into an unsafe position. **Webster the Spider** (Fisher-Price) is a friendly, brightly colored spider that wiggles its eight legs when a short string is pulled.

Stimulate Various Senses **Baby Play Gyms** (Childcraft; Toys to Grow On) are for the child who is able to sit up and crawl. **Gymfinity** (Today's Kids) dangles black-and-white animals on large colorful links in a baby-gym configuration. Later, toddlers can enjoy the activity panel (with gears, puzzles, and sorters) that is built into the unit.

Spinner Rattle (Johnson & Johnson) rattles as it changes colors and spins. The rattle is easily manipulated by an infant, and its red ring doubles as a handle and a teether. **Voice-Activated Crib Mobile** (Johnson & Johnson) encourages your baby to vocalize; a baby's chatter or cry activates this colorful musical mobile and causes stars to rotate above the crib. **Dancing Animals Music Box Mobile** (Fisher-Price) combines music, color, and motion.

Various spinners and push toys combine sight and sound and have the added benefit of inviting your baby to manipulate the toy and create an action-reaction sequence. **Corn Popper** (Fisher-Price) produces sound when rolled, as brightly colored balls pop inside a see-through dome; **Poppin' Top** (Ohio Art) creates something of the same effect in a "top" form.

Learn to Play An infant does not play with items by instinct. All children must be taught to play. The adult who is interacting with an infant nearly always does so as a teacher—showing a child how things work by working them . . .

causing the top to spin . . . blowing a mobile into motion. As a teaching adult, express a sense of joy and delight as you demonstrate a new toy or expose an infant to new stimuli.

Words of Caution

1. Use only new products. Avoid old toys that might have lead paint on them. Also avoid soft plastic toys, pacifiers, and teethers manufactured before the mid-1980s; many were manufactured with DEHP, a chemical now considered hazardous to the health of an infant. (Some products manufactured in other countries still use DEHP. Buy American!)

2. Make certain that all items you use for play with your baby have components that cannot be swallowed or aspirated, and that they have no jagged or sharp edges.

3. Position a mobile so that your infant can't reach it.

4. Do not leave toys unattended in the crib of an infant. The day will come when your baby is able to reach out and grab it for himself and immediately attempt to chew on it. Remove all toys attached to a baby's crib or playpen as soon as she is able to push herself up on hands and knees (at about five months).

5. Do not purchase crib toys with strings longer than twelve inches.

6. Choose infant toys that are washable (with hot water and soap for sterilization).

2 ◆ BabyCise

BabyCise (Matchbox Toys) is a complete exercise system for babies. It includes foam blocks, bolsters, and playmats that can be arranged in various shapes. A video demonstrates a series of safety-tested activities using the equipment.

Advantage The chief advantage of BabyCise is that it invites a baby and a parent to work together in the exercises—creating fun, bonding moments, even as the baby's muscle tone and coordination abilities are developed.

Play Environment Always remember that your child's favorite "toy" is going to be *you*. Babies, especially, covet your closeness, your involvement, your voice, your touch. BabyCise creates a framework in which you and your baby can play together in a productive, stimulating manner—and, thus, an environment in which you can teach your baby how to play.

3 ◆ Blocks

Blocks have been around as a toy for nearly three hundred years. In the early nineteenth century, the founder of modern kindergartens, Friedrich Froebel, was the first to suggest blocks in different shapes as building units for making creative structures. Prior to that time, blocks were used mainly to teach the alphabet and spelling.

Blocks today—as well as various nesting and stacking toys—come in a wide variety of materials for virtually all ages of children. These durable, creative toys teach your child the elements of building—balance, eye-hand coordination, the properties of shape and size.

Nonwooden Blocks **Soft Blocks** (Galt) and **Jingle Blocks** (Toys to Grow On) are made of foam, covered with washable fabric. The Galt set has six blocks, each printed on all sides with bright colorful designs; the Toys to Grow On blocks have a jingling mechanism embedded in them and come in sets of eight. This type of block spans the ages four months to four years.

Foam Blocks (Marlon Creations) float in the water and are easily handled by a baby. The blocks—which come in various sizes, colors, and shapes—can be used as sponges and stampers, and since they stick together when wet, they can be a bathtub building set.

Tyco Preschool Super Blocks (Tyco) snap together; the blocks are made of brightly colored plastic and are packaged in carry-along containers. (Tyco blocks are compatible with Lego blocks.) **Waffle Blocks** (Little Tikes), made of nontoxic polyethylene, come in bright primary colors and three sizes: Wee Waffle Blocks (for creating structures on a table or floor), Waffle Blocks (eight-inch blocks, for building larger structures on the floor), and Big Waffle Blocks (for putting together child-sized playhouses).

Blockbusters (Brrr Products), shoe-box-sized blocks made of lightweight material, can be stacked to create child-sized hideouts and forts.

Sorting Blocks (Brio Scanditoy) come as a set with blocks of various shapes and sizes in primary colors along with a wooden tray for building and storage. **Duplo Blocks** (Lego) are available in assorted models and various sets; these hand-sized plastic building blocks lock together easily.

Wooden Blocks   These blocks are produced by virtually all mainstream toy manufacturers and specialty manufacturers. Those by Galt, Childcraft, and Toys to Grow On are made of fine-quality hardwood (unpainted) and come in various sets. Wooden blocks generally are recommended for children at least two years old.

Letter Wood Blocks (Playskool) are embossed with letters and numbers. During play, the shapes of letters and numbers are reinforced. Blocks can be placed vertically or horizontally to form simple words.

Sign Blocks (available through National Association of the Deaf) are sturdy wooden blocks that have letters, pictures, and the corresponding finger configurations in sign language.

Nesting Cubes (Little Tikes) can be used for stacking, storing, or nesting. This toy encourages a child to experiment with size and sharpens her ability to discriminate between smaller and larger items. **Stacking Toys** (Brio Scanditoy) invite a toddler to stack, order, and combine objects of varying shapes. **Stack and Fit School** (Johnson & Johnson) is a set of plastic nesting blocks and tubes for stacking and building. While creating towers, the child develops eye-hand coordination and learns about shapes.

Galaxy Magnetic Spheres (Childcraft) give a twist to playing with blocks. Four size-graduated spheres and a solid ball are magnetized so that the child may form numerous combinations of shapes.

Words of Caution

1. Make certain that the blocks are free of lead paint.

2. Determine that all pieces in a set of blocks are too large for an infant to swallow.

3. Keep batteries from small children; they pose a potential choking and toxicity hazard.

4 ◆ Little People Playsets

The **Little People Playsets** (Fisher-Price) have become a mainstay in the toyboxes of children two to six years old. Several sets are available.

Garage Playset A three-level parking garage has a gas pump, parking meter, hydrant, phone, grease rack, car elevator, moving stop signs, ringing bell, and a crank that rotates the platform. It comes with four Little People figures and three cars.

Main Street An entire play village is made up of a grocery store, an ice cream shop, a post office, a pet shop, a fire house (with bell and fire truck), a drive-through bank, and a barbershop. Various ramps combine to form roadways. The set comes with five Little People figures, two vehicles, and six street accessories.

Other playsets include a Jetliner, Airport, Farm, Home, and Zoo.

The foremost advantage of these playsets is that they invite children to create story lines using the various props and people figures. Conflicts inevitably occur in such stories and can be resolved as a part of play—thus helping a child develop conflict-resolution skills. The playsets are rooted in a real world yet permit a child to imagine and to take on various roles.

Words of Caution

1. The Little People figurines were recently re-designed so that they cannot be ingested by infants. Buy new playsets (or ones manufactured after the redesign).

2. The Little People Jetliner comes with a cord so that it can be a pull toy. Detach the cord before the toy is used in a playpen or crib.

5 ♦ Pounding Toys

Pounding toys are classic toddler toys. They develop eye-hand coordination and teach a child about cause-and-effect relationships.

Pound the Pegs! **Baby Pounding Bench** (Playskool) is made of plastic and shaped like a deep dish on freestanding molded legs. After the child pounds down the three pegs of varying shapes with the plastic mallet, he can turn the unit over and pound the pegs back from the other side. The **Flip Flop Tool Box** (Little Tikes) operates by the same principle; the only difference is that the unit is shaped like a tool box.

Swing That Hammer! **Hammer the Beads** (Brio Scanditoy) is a wooden toy with three balls to hit. When hit with a large wooden mallet, each ball pops out of the hole at the end of the chute. **Bang-A-Ball** (Childcraft) is similar but is made of plastic. It has four colorful balls and a mallet in a toy configured like a circular chute. When the child bangs the balls, they come out through various openings at the base of the cylinder.

The traditional **Cobbler's Bench** (Playskool) is

made of wood with pegs and mallet. A similar version, with balls instead of pegs, is available through Toys to Grow On: a child pounds a jumbo ball through a hole and then watches the ball roll down a ramp and out the side of the bench-shaped unit.

Word of Caution   Make certain that all pieces of a set are too large for a baby to ingest.

6 ◆ Ride-On Toys

From swings to rocking horses to bikes, children love ride-on toys! Be sure to choose a toy that the child must power.

Swing **Toddler Swing** (Little Tikes) is made of molded plastic and designed to securely and comfortably hold a toddler. The child is able to propel the lightweight swing on his own, thus developing gross motor skills and arm and leg coordination. As in the case of all swings, a suitable anchoring device must be used to ensure stability.

Cars **Rocking Car** (Childcraft) is an updated version of the old rocking horse. When attached to a rocking device (included in the set), the car is a rocker. When removed from the rocker, it is a car that runs on foot power.

Cozy Coupe (Little Tikes) looks like a real car (in the VW Bug tradition) and guides and controls like a vehicle with a steering wheel. It is operated by foot power.

Trikes   Choose a **Tricycle** (numerous manufacturers) with a contoured seat, nonslip foot pedals, large sturdy wheels, and easy-to-grasp handles. See the new heavy gauge molded plastic one from Little Tikes. The one offered by Childcraft has a push-button horn and a carrying basket on back. **Tiny Trike** (Galt) is made of wood and has dual front wheels for added stability. **My First Trike** (Toys to Grow On) has fat spokeless poly wheels with rubber treads for good traction and safety; it's well proportioned for tots as young as eighteen months.

Combinations   **Baby Sit 'n' Walk** (Childcraft) is a clever adaptation of a ride-on toy. It becomes a walker when pushed and doubles as a chair with six activities. **Happy Locomotive** (Childcraft) is another ride-on toy and walker combination.

Rocking Animals   A **Rocking Horse** or **Bouncing Horse** (or other animal) should be sturdy, and the springs should be covered to avoid pinching little fingers and toes. One of the finest rocking horses is by Toys to Grow On; the back support/armrest can be used for infants and then unscrewed in minutes for toddlers. The horse swings smoothly and quietly while the platform remains steady, so it can't tip over. It's not inexpensive but is of heirloom quality. The **Baby Rocking Horse** (Childcraft) is designed like a chair, with ridged handlebars, an adjustable safety belt, and footrests.

Rocking Puppy (Fisher-Price) rocks without tipping; low to the ground, it allows the young rider to get on and off safely and independently.

Truck **Husky Hauler Dump Truck** (Coleco) is something of a bridge between a tricycle and a bicycle. This vehicle, made of lightweight plastic, has four small, wide rear wheels and one large front wheel attached to a steering column.

Bikes and Skateboards   **Bicycles** and **Skateboards** attract children five years and over. Numerous manufacturers have given consumers lots of choices of model, style, and design. Choose a bike that has growing room for your child. When dealing with skateboards, check the messages sometimes imprinted on them. And above all, when your children move into bicycle and skateboard activities, insist that they don appropriate helmets and shoulder and knee pads. **Rollerboard** (The Right Start Catalog) is safe as a scooter, but it has the look, feel, and action of a skateboard. It is especially for the four- to seven-year-old set.

Word of Caution   Three-wheel and four-wheel off-road vehicles are *not* for children!

7 ◆ Wagons

Whether used as a carriage for dolls, as a transportation means for a younger brother or sister, as a hauling vehicle for rocks, blocks, or toys, or as a storage container, the little red wagon is still a favorite of children.

Classic Designs   It's tough to beat the classic **Radio Flyer** red wagon with molded wheels.

The **Wagon** (John Deere—yes, the tractor manufacturer) is an extremely well-made metal version of the classic hay wagon—in green, however. You can also get a two-wheel tag-along wagon that attaches to the main wagon for hauling extra loads.

First Wagons   **Toddler Wagon** (Little Tikes) is a good first wagon. Made of durable molded plastic, it has a handle wide enough for two-handed pushing. The stable wheel base and a fixed handle ensure few spills or turnovers.

Baby Walker (Galt) is actually a push-style wagon with a 22 1/2-inch vertical-style handle and a low-to-the-ground carrying box. Made of hardwood, with steel tires and rubber tread, it is extremely sturdy and not easily tipped over.

Word of Caution Look for rustproof wagons that stand up to both outdoor and indoor use.

8 ♦ Toy Telephones

Children like to talk on the phone. Play telephone sets encourage a child's conversational ability as the child makes up dialogue (sometimes both parts).

For the Younger Set **Chatter Telephone** (Fisher-Price) is a telephone pull toy that produces a chattering sound; its eyes roll when pulled, and a bell rings when the dial is turned.

Small plastic princess-style and regular-style phones are available from several manufacturers. Children seem to enjoy dial-style units just as much as push buttons. Choose one that "rings" when dialed!

Small Talk (Childcraft) is an upscale version of the toy telephone. The phone has six buttons with animals, ten buttons with numbers and people, and an eight-note piano-style keyboard. Press the animal buttons to hear animal sounds. A computer-style voice tells about colors, shapes, and numbers, or how to play music on the keyboard. Made of plastic, it requires batteries. A similar unit, **Talking Phone** (Hasbro), has messages from familiar characters such as Mickey Mouse and Big Bird.

For the Older Set   Older children will enjoy a phone set similar to a walkie-talkie. Connect their rooms with lifelike phone units (joined by wire), and let them ring up one another.

Or you can resort to **Walkie Talkies** (AT&T). With a range of three hundred feet, this set features a press-to-talk button, flexible antenna, solid-state amplifier, and speaker; each has fifteen buttons to send Morse code messages (requires two nine-volt batteries). A similar set called **Sky Talkers Walkie Talkies** (Fisher-Price) has oversized knobs and recessed controls (again, nine-volt batteries are required).

Word of Caution   Keep any phone cords, batteries, or strings out of cribs and playpens. Batteries may pose a toxicity hazard.

9 ◆ Vehicles

Toy cars and trucks are for boys *and* girls.

Tonka Trucks (Tonka Toys) Highly durable steel construction and very realistic—lots of detail! —these vehicles can be used in independent play, in dramatic group play, and in combination with other playthings (*see chapter 10*). The toy line includes dune buggies to eighteen-wheelers to car-carrier trucks with cars that can be removed. The **Mighty Tonka Crane** (also known as "Lift It") is an oversized toy crane that allows children to fill, lift, rotate, and unload gravel, dirt, and sand; the **Mighty Tonka Dump** (also known as "Dump It") allows children to transport and dump loads; and the **Mighty Tonka Loader** (also known as "Scoop It"), a loader with a bucket, scoops, dumps, and hauls.

Tractors John Deere makes toy tractors and antique replicas from cast metal, painted with child-safe enamel. The vehicles have moving parts and real steering.

Workers' Vehicles   Digger Dan's Construction Co. Colossal Crane (Ceiji-Revell) is a large crane toy with six remote-control functions for sandbox or backyard play.

Classic Aerial Hook-N-Ladder (Nylint) is a large fire-fighting vehicle with a ladder that extends and revolves 360 degrees.

Wooden Vehicles   Marvel has a line of Wooden Vehicles: a flatbed truck, a sedan, a pickup, a jeep, and an airplane.

Miniature Diecast Vehicles   Those by Matchbox are of diecast metal. The cars are child-hand-sized and have doors that hinge open, hoods that lift up, and other parts that move. All have rolling wheels, but none has detachable parts. Highly realistic in their design, they are fairly inexpensive (under five dollars each, usually). Similar in design are Hot Wheels Cars (Mattel) and Majorette Mini-Cars (Majorette). Some of the Mattel designs are "fantasy cars" as well as noncar vehicles such as fire engines and construction machinery. Some of the Mattel and Majorette cars have detachable parts.

Words of Caution
1. These toy vehicles are not recommended for children under three years of age.
2. Generally speaking, I do *not* recommend battery-operated or remote-control vehicles.

10 ◆ Transportation Systems

Transportation systems are available for trains, cars, and boats.

Railways The beginner set of the **Brio Wooden Railway System** (Brio Scanditoy) has eight curved pieces of track, an engine, and cargo cars. Additional accessories include lengths of track, bridge supports, and so forth—even houses and buildings to line the track. Made of unpainted wood, the system is highly durable and allows for flexibility in design. T. C. Timber manufactures a similar **Wooden Railway Set** for children two years and older.

Roadways **Creative Roadway** (Little Tikes) is a plastic roadway set with large easy-to-connect sections. The set includes a bridge and tunnel, two buildings, a car, and a wagon.

Busy Beads (Playskool) is a wire unit along which beads roll—teaching children some of the basic principles of momentum. **Roller Coaster** (Anatex) is a similar unit, as is the **Curves and Waves** (Anatex) set.

Marble Run (Lillian Vernon) has forty-eight

bright interlocking plastic sections that combine to create chutes, bridges, pillars, and hoppers down which a marble can roll. The set comes with twelve marbles.

Waterways **Aquaplay Canal System** (Galt) is a component system that has six curves and one straight section, one harbor piece, two boats (one is a towing barge), and a paddlewheel. After the sections are linked together by watertight connecting fasteners, the unit is filled with water. When the child turns the paddlewheel, a current moves the boats around the canal.

Waterway (Discovery Toys) and **Tike Waterway** (Little Tikes) are similar systems. Such systems capture the imagination of children as young as two years old. The systems are good for both indoor and outdoor play. **Tubtown Sea Circus** (Lakeside) is a tub toy that has an underwater circus motif with floating dolphins, rescue boats, and a working elevator.

Words of Caution

1. I do *not* recommend electric train or car sets for the young child. Creativity, motor skills, and group dynamics are all enhanced by leaving the movement of the units under a child's control. Furthermore, the use of electricity poses a potential hazard for young children.

2. Make sure all young children are closely supervised so that they do not choke on any small component parts.

11 ◆ Dolls

Children virtually always see dolls as their own babies, putting themselves in the parenting role. Dolls provide a valuable means of role-model training and an outlet for play related to behaviors the children will carry into adulthood.

Stuffed Dolls From the age of three, a toddler enjoys an oversized stuffed doll with jointed limbs, rooted hair, and shiny eyes, such as **My Child Doll** (Mattel). She comes with a disposable diaper, brush, comb, and "brag book" (for recording information about the doll). Extra diapers, accessories, and clothing are sold separately. The doll is machine washable. **Real Baby** (Hasbro) looks and feels like a genuine baby.

My Buddy (Playskool) is a twenty-one-inch toddler boy doll that has shiny rooted hair, a machine washable stuffed body, and eyes that open and close. He comes dressed in overalls, polo shirt, baseball cap, and sneakers. I heartily recommend him for both boys and girls.

Toddlers and young children do not need numerous dolls. Give your child the opportunity to pick out a doll within your price range.

Heirloom Dolls The **American Girl** (in three designs) and **American Baby** (in three designs) dolls are beautifully fashioned and come with a full line of accessories. These dolls, as well as the baby dolls manufactured by Madame Alexandria, are expensive but timeless in design. They are definitely for the older child.

Rubber and Vinyl Dolls **Pliable People** (Childcraft) are soft rubber dolls that stay in the position in which they are posed. They come as sets, with a mother, father, and three children, and are scaled for play with blocks. (Childcraft also offers **Wooden Figure Sets,** similar to paper dolls, for use with their blocks.)

My Bathable Baby (Fisher-Price) is a soft vinyl doll that a child can take to the bathtub. **Softina** (Childcraft) and **Baby Paul** (Carolle) are similar dolls.

Environments offers ten thirteen-inch washable vinyl dolls—five boys and five girls—in Hispanic, Asian, African-American, Caucasian, and American Indian models. **Just-Born Babies** also come in both boy and girl models and in various ethnic models: African-American, Asian, Hispanic, Native American, and Caucasian. These are anatomically correct dolls. **Multi-Ethnic Dolls** (Childcraft) are sturdy vinyl boy and girl dolls in Hispanic, Asian, Caucasian, and African-American models.

"Teaching" Dolls   **Dapper Dan and Dressy Bessy** (Playskool) and **Buttons & Toes** (Fisher-Price) help a child develop the ability to button buttons, zip zippers, tie laces, and snap snaps.

Paper Dolls   Paper dolls are now available in a variety of sets—from highly detailed costume sets of the past to modern fashions. They are most appropriate for the older child, who has sufficient hand-eye coordination to manipulate pointed scissors.

Words of Caution

1. Dolls for young children should be washable. After washing, check all seams to make sure they are secure. Children five years and under should be supervised during play because small parts are a potential choking hazard.

2. Be cautious in encouraging a young child to play with paper dolls. Young children should use only blunt-nosed scissors, which are often insufficient for the detailing of paper dolls.

3. I am a little hesitant in my recommendation about anatomically correct dolls as a norm for play. These dolls can be very helpful, however, if a parent chooses to teach a child lessons about sexual anatomy or behavior. A doll should foster loving, nurturing care in a child, not questions about sex.

4. When shopping for a doll, keep in mind the child's skill level. Young children will find tiny snaps and buttons on doll clothing extremely frustrating.

5. Perhaps as important as the dolls that I recommend are the dolls that I do *not* recommend.

- I do *not* recommend Barbie (Mattel) or her friends.

    These adult-figured dolls, in my opinion, cause a girl to develop unrealistic expectations about her future. The play associated with these dolls is that of dating and teenage relationships—inappropriate play for a four-year-old. Even a cocreator of the Barbie doll later expressed his concerns about the doll and refused to provide one for his grandchildren!

- I do *not* recommend Jem (Hasbro), She-Ra (Mattel), My Little Pony (Hasbro), or any doll associated with a television series.

    Such dolls come with preprogrammed play. A child who watches the related program comes to the doll with an idea about what the doll is supposed to do. That thwarts a child's creative involvement with the doll. Let children make up their own stories and give each doll a unique personality, which may very well change from hour to hour.

    In addition, some action-figure characters (such as She-Ra) possess occult powers and engage in violent activity on their related television programs—behaviors that most adults do not want to encourage or reinforce in their children.

- I do *not* recommend male action-figure dolls, either.

  The G.I. Joe dolls aren't what they used to be! Many action-figure dolls are associated with television programs and electronic gadgetry—making them preprogrammed, violent, *and* expensive. The same goes for He-Man and his cohorts.

  As for Teenage Mutant Ninja Turtles . . . I have no desire for my young son to mutate or to become a ninja. The related movies and television series have numerous examples of ninja philosophy (a highly violent Eastern religion), and again, the toys come preprogrammed for play.

- Finally, I do *not* recommend Cabbage Patch Dolls (Coleco).

  These dolls, which come with their own name and adoption papers, place too great a sense of responsibility on the young child.

12 ◆ Doll Accessories

With dolls comes a desire for doll accessories!

Buggy **Doll Buggy** (Little Tikes), made of molded polyethylene, has a solid circular handle and oversized nonremovable wheels.

Cradle **Doll Cradle** (Childcraft) has a pink-and-white tufted mattress and pillow; it is made of white enamel accented with shiny brass and has a gentle rocking action.

Dollhouses **Dollhouses,** especially those with miniature accessories, are generally for the older child. An increasing number of young child sets are appearing on the market, however. **Colonial Doll House** (Childcraft) has five rooms of unpainted hardwood, ready for your child to furnish and decorate. The furniture, also of unpainted wood, tends to be blocky. Flexible wooden dolls may be ordered (including grandparents, a family of five, and a nurse and doctor).

One of the most elaborate dollhouses for the younger child is the **Victorian Dream House** (Toys to Grow On) that has five rooms, an attic, and a patio. It comes decorated with doors and windows that open and shut, and three play figures. Best of all, it's made of durable plastic. The house snaps together and, thus, can be stored away. A set of more than one hundred pieces of furniture and props can be ordered.

Playsets   **Doll Care Center** (Childcraft) has a changing table and everything a child needs for the care of a favorite doll—cooking table with sink and stove, built-in high chair, and twenty-seven accessories (from brush to baby bottle). **Deluxe Vanity Set** (Childcraft) comes with a vanity mirror and chair in which a doll may sit; lots of accessories accompany the set. Both sets are made of highly durable plastic and are easily assembled.

School Days Doll Set (Childcraft) is a twelve-piece playset that includes small desks, chairs, a blackboard, and a classroom environment as well as four five-inch children and a teacher.

The **American Girl Doll** (and the **American Baby**) series comes with a full line of accessories, including books that have stories featuring the "girls" after which the dolls are fashioned. Clothing, furniture, tea sets, and so forth are available.

Don't overlook the play value of a **Tea Party Set.** Doll-sized teapot, plates, cups, and saucers can provide hours of fun. Beautiful sets are made by many manufacturers, including some by the producers of fine china. Plastic sets are best for young children, however. (This is an item to scout out at a flea market or garage sale.)

Virtually all doll paraphernalia and sets take up a lot of space. You may want to consider a small shelving unit as a make-believe dollhouse for your child. Later, books or other items can be stored on the shelves.

Words of Caution

1. Some doll paraphernalia designed for larger dolls so closely resembles real-baby accessories that it can present a real danger if used inappropriately for infants. Toy strollers, infant seats (the kind that hook onto tables), high chairs, and back carriers are *not* designed to hold the weight or activity of a real baby.

2. Small accessory items—and especially miniatures related to dollhouses—should be kept out of the reach of children five years and under. They pose a definite choking hazard.

13 ◆ Shape Sorters

Nearly every young child enjoys sorting objects and exploring the ways in which objects fit together. Sorting toys enable the child to develop tactile discrimination skills and eye-hand and small muscle coordination.

Keys and Things **Key Sorter** (Kapable Kids) has five colorful keys with different-shaped ends. When placed in the appropriate slot and turned, each key triggers a different sound, sight, or action.

My Shape 'N' Stir Pot (Playskool) comes with nine colorful plastic shapes. The shapes are pushed through corresponding cutouts in the pot's top and then can be mixed with a large teethable mixing spoon. **Shape Sorter** (Tupperware) has a reversible lid that accommodates a child's growth in coordination. **Shape-O-Toy** (Tupperware) is a ball/rattle for babies, a shape sorter for toddlers, and a numbers/counting toy for preschoolers.

Shape Sorter Transporter (Johnson & Johnson) is a plastic truck; it houses large pegs that can be sorted and stacked on molded stands, which appear when the truck's hatch doors are opened.

Primary Shape Sorter has fifty-four colorful rubber pieces (six each of nine shapes) that stack up on nine posts on a wooden base.

Posting Box (Brio Scanditoy) is made of wood. Colorful shapes are dropped through the slots of a square post office box.

Houses and Things Sorting House (Discovery Toys) requires a child to place different-shaped objects into a house with cutout slots. **Gazebo Shape and Sort Key House** (Chicco) has colorful doors that can be opened with a matching color key to reveal a friendly animal shape.

Little Lighthouse Toy (Tupperware) is a three-dimensional plastic lighthouse puzzle requiring both size and shape discrimination skills. Graduated pieces have hollow interiors of varying shapes. As the pieces are stacked together to form a completed lighthouse, the toy rocks on a sealed base.

Learning Garage (Lillian Vernon) is a three-door garage unit with three cars. Children must shape- and color-match a key to a closed garage door, then press a button before a garage door will open. The garage has a skylight for viewing the cars.

14 ◆ Stuffed Animals

The classic stuffed animal is a bear named Teddy. The tradition began in 1902, when President Theodore "Teddy" Roosevelt took a trip to the South. For recreation, Roosevelt engaged in a hunting expedition. To make certain that the president returned home with a hunting trophy, the expedition hosts trapped a bear cub for him to kill, but Roosevelt refused to fire.

A cartoon of the incident was drawn by Clifford Berryman and carried in the *Washington Star*. It inspired a toy salesman in Brooklyn, Morris Michtom, to make a stuffed bear cub. Michtom put the cartoon and the cub in his toy store window and invited customers to purchase their own "Teddy's Bear." Michtom eventually formed the Ideal Toy Company.

About the same time, Margaret Steiff, who headed a prosperous toy company in Germany, saw the illustration and created her own plush version of the bear, which was a great hit at the 1904 Leipzig Fair. The stuffed bears quickly became the most popular toys of the era, and they were frequently dressed with sweaters, jackets, or overcoats.

The company founded by Margaret Steiff is still one of the finest plush toy manufacturers in the world. Steiff offers a wide range of stuffed animals and dolls, featuring realistic-looking cats, tigers, puppies, monkeys, and other animals. They range in price from thirty dollars to limited edition creations costing up to one thousand dollars.

Another fine stuffed animal manufacturer is Gund. More moderately priced than Steiff, the Gund line ranges from hand puppets to a collectible series. Again, the animals are highly realistic.

In purchasing a plush toy, check for these elements:

Quality Construction The hair, whiskers, and eyes should be secured firmly. Any bows, ribbons, or other decorative items should be stitched tightly to the toy.

Washability Plush toys to be cuddled by babies and young toddlers must be washable. After washing, check seams carefully to make certain they are secure. Escaping "stuffing" poses a choking hazard.

Chemical Smell If you detect any type of chemical odor, leave the toy on the store's shelf. U.S. government standards prohibit the use of chemicals in toy manufacturing, but some imported toys (especially those from the Orient) contain traceable amounts of petroleum-based chemicals.

Type of Stuffing   Some plush toys are stuffed with plastic pellets, chopped walnut shells, and beans. If any of these escape through a crack or tear in the fabric, they pose a serious choking hazard. Look for toys with foam, polyester, or natural fiber stuffing.

Interior Wires   Squeeze a plush toy to check for interior wires that could cut or puncture your child's skin if they protrude accidentally.

The foremost factors to consider with a plush toy are its softness and "cuddle-ability." Let your child cradle several plush toys in a toy store before you make your selection.

Words of Caution

1. I do *not* recommend Teddy Ruxpin (Worlds of Wonder) or any toys that have tape recorders or battery-prompted animation. Let your child give voice to the plush toy!

2. I do *not* recommend toys linked to television programs, including Care Bears (Kenner), Alf (Coleco), Furskins (Coleco), Garfield (Dakin), Popples (Mattel), Rainbow Brite Dolls (Mattel), and so forth.

3. I do *not* recommend fantasy-style stuffed animals. Plenty of realistic plush toys are available without resorting to monsters or outer space goblins.

4. After washing a stuffed toy, make certain eyes, trim, and other small items that may present a choking hazard are attached securely.

15 ◆ Balls

A ball is likely to be the toy that your child will enjoy the most consistently from infancy to adulthood. It is perhaps the most universal of all playthings.

First Balls   **Chime Ball** (Princess Soft Toys) is small and light enough to be handled or swatted comfortably by a baby. When the ball is pushed or rolled, it emits a chime sound. The multicolored ball stimulates eye movement and develops color discrimination skills.

Clutch Ball (Galt) is made of soft washable vinyl. Four inches in diameter, it has deep indentations designed especially for little fingers (as young as six months).

"Magic" Balls   **Magic Catch Mitts** (Synergistics) and **No-Fail Catch Game** (Toys to Grow On) both allow a young child to catch a Velcro-covered ball without a great deal of small muscle development or eye-hand coordination. The balls stick to the disk-shaped plastic mitts that have adjustable hand straps.

Foam Balls **Lunar Balls** (Childcraft) are non-toxic foam balls that come in various sizes and colors for both indoor and outdoor play.

Nerf Balls (Parker) are favorites for children six years and older. Made of soft "Nerf foam," the balls are designed to minimize injuries often associated with regulation sport balls.

Giant Balls Giant **Activity Balls** are ideal toys for helping a child develop muscle coordination and balance. The Childcraft version of these balls ranges in diameter from sixteen to thirty-seven inches, and their **Jumping Balls** (with a handle, of sorts, that encourages children to sit on the balls and bounce) range in size from fifteen to twenty-one inches in diameter.

Physioball and **Gymnastik Ball** (available through Equipment Shop and some specialty catalogs) are molded vinyl balls measuring up to fifty inches in diameter. They are often used in physical therapy but are enjoyed by all children. **Hoppity Hop Ball** (Sun Products) and **Big Bounce** (Discovery Toys) are similar items to the Jumping Balls.

Words of Caution

1. As for all toys with a spongelike consistency, balls made of soft spongy material (such as Nerf Balls) should be kept away from children five years and under unless closely supervised. A

young child may bite off a small piece of the ball and choke.

2. Choose balls appropriate for the age and muscle coordination level of your child.

16 ◆ "Play School" Items

"Let's play school" is something young children love to do, even after coming home from a full day of the real thing. These items are long on promoting creativity and individuality and short on cost.

Math Helps   You might have to look long and hard for an **Abacus**—the ancient Chinese adding machine. Check a "learning shop," or ask your child's teacher about the possibility of ordering through a school supply catalog. The child-appropriate abacus will be one with different colors for each row of balls or disks. **Counting Frame** (Sanberg) is recommended for children two to six years old.

Show your child how to use an abacus for making simple calculations. For many children, seeing the numbers take shape and counting them make mathematics much more tangible and much easier to comprehend.

Number Scale (Childcraft) is a friendly clown-faced "scale" that asks children to balance numbers by weight. The numbers that are hung on the balance-beam scale are graduated in size and weight. A "2" and a "3," for example, must be hung on one side of the scale to equal the weight of the "5." The scale comes with fourteen weighted numbers made of durable plastic.

Chalkboard You might opt for a hand-held model (also known as a slate). Toys to Grow On offers a 15 1/2-by-18 1/2-inch model with a wooden frame. On the back of the chalkboard is a magnetic board. (The set comes with thirty-six magnetic letters and numbers.) Provide plenty of chalk and a good eraser.

Wide-Ruled School Paper and Chubby-Finger Pencils Ruled newsprint is still the favorite for school pads. Pencils should be easy to grasp (no longer than seven to eight inches). Don't forget a pencil sharpener.

Desk **Alpha Desk** (Today's Kids) is a bright molded plastic freestanding unit—one piece—that has a lift-top lid for storing supplies. It is designed for children ages two to five.

Typewriter **Petite 990 Typewriter** (Britain's Petite, Inc.) is a child-sized typewriter with real keys, a standardized keyboard, and other adult-machine features. A manual, it uses reversible carbon ribbons in "no-mess" cassettes. This working toy can teach typing skills at an early age. (In this age of computers, knowing how to type on keyboards can be a critical skill!)

17 ◆ "Play Kitchen" Items

"Playing kitchen" prepares children for an inevitable fact of adulthood—the need to cook. The best props for the preschooler are realistic and familiar.

Everything Including the Kitchen Sink
A Child's Dream Kitchen (Little Tikes) includes highly realistic, separate child-sized plastic appliances—**Stove, Sink,** and **Refrigerator.**

"Play With Me" Sink 'N' Stove (Wolverine Toys) is a portable version of a play kitchen. The hinged sink and stove close together to create a box with handles that make the unit travelworthy.

Kitchen Appliances (Childcraft) are scaled-down units made of plywood with Formica tops, warp-proof doors, and magnetic door catches. Available are a refrigerator, sink, stove, and dutch-style cabinet. Constructive Playthings has a line of **Wooden Playsets** including a refrigerator, stove, oven, pantry, and telephone booth.

Little Tikes' **Play Kitchen** is versatile and compact. The molded plastic freestanding set has representative units for cooking and storage—with utensils and fake food items. A wall phone hangs on its side.

Pots and Pans Along with the kitchen units, a child needs pots and pans. You might opt for plastic ones in varying sizes (such as those available from Toys to Grow On). With **Let's Cook** (Galt), a child gets a saucepan and fitted lid, frying pan, colander, calibrated measuring cup, mixing bowl, wooden spoon, and spatula. The pans are made of spun aluminum.

Dishes Don't forget dishes! Plastic tableware and utensils can be purchased from toy manufacturers, or use shatterproof family discards.

Food Toys to Grow On manufactures a set of thirty-eight pieces of vinyl play food in six stackable plastic crates—from milk and juice to pastry items to vegetables and fruits.

Baking Supplies Eventually, your child will have a desire to embark on learning the real thing. Klutz offers a children's cookbook with recipes for things children like to make and eat.

Pastry cutters are a big hit with children—for cookies as well as Play-Doh creations. The plastic cutters from Galt are in the shapes of a dog, rabbit, star, steam engine, and gingerbread family (in three sizes).

Easy-Bake Brownie and Cookie Set (Kenner) has three small bags of real brownie mix and three of real cookie mix, a measuring spoon, pan, and child-sized mixing bowl.

18 ◆ Bubble Makers

Children love bubbles—the more the merrier. And the bubble industry is becoming more and more creative to meet their demands.

Bubbles to Go **Bubble-Danglers** (Toys to Grow On) come as a set of four small decorative bottles filled with neon-colored bubble mix, sweetly scented, that have colorful cords attached so that a vial can be worn as a necklace. The wand is built into the cap of the vial.

Big Bubbles **Giant Bubble Machine** (Toys to Grow On) is a bubble-blowing version of a squirt gun. Fill the small dish with giant bubble mix (both included in the set), dip the nozzle of the bubble machine in the solution, and pull the trigger. Gently pull the trigger once and you'll create a giant bubble. Squeeze quickly with pressure and you'll create a string of small bubbles. (The unit requires two AA batteries.)

Bubble Wands (Childcraft) come in a set with four 28 1/4-inch-long plastic wands; each has a different "head" with designs including hearts, circles, planets and stars, and swirls.

Mega Bubble (John Deere and other specialty catalogs) has an extra large (ten inches in diameter) bubble wand that comes with a *Bubbleology Guide*. Klutz makes a similar wand and book set with lots of ideas for making strange-shaped, super-sized bubbles.

Bubble Machines
Bubble Mower (Fisher-Price) is a plastic child-sized lawn mower that can be filled with bubble solution. When the mower is pushed, it emits a string of bubbles and makes a realistic sound.

With the **Bubble Camera** (Mattel), children aim and "shoot" a picture, and a bubble comes out the "lens."

Bubble Juice
Childcraft offers a fifty-ounce **Barrel of Bubbles** for about five dollars.

You can make bubbles with materials you probably already have. For a wand, use a unit of plastic rings that links together a six-pack of canned soft drinks.

Words of Caution
1. Bubble mix should be kept away from young children.

2. The Giant Bubble Machine should be used by children five years and older; batteries can pose both a potential choking and a toxicity hazard for young children.

3. Bubble-Dangler cords should be kept away from small children.

19 ◆ Construction Sets

Every child enjoys a building set.

Plastic Sets Lego is the name that most readily comes to mind for children over the age of three. Lego "bricks" are colorful plastic snap-together units packaged with a variety of accessories. The Lego blocks come in a wide range of sizes, from a fraction of an inch to two inches and more in diameter. In addition to the **Basic Building Set,** specialty sets capture the imagination of older children.

- **Lego Town Sets** permit the young builder to create a town.
- **Legoland Space Sets** have components specially designed to build space stations.
- **Lego Technic** is an entire line of more complex building sets for older children to use in constructing detailed vehicles.

Brick Vac (Lego) comes with 131 Lego pieces, but the best part is that the storage unit "picks up" after play is over! When a child rolls the unit over the bricks, its plastic paddles scoop them up.

(Some Lego sets include battery-powered components, although batteries aren't included.)

Ramagon (Ramagon) offers snap-together units with a ball-and-strut design. Each unit has twenty-six connection points for flexibility in design. The units are compatible with Lego bricks.

Bristle Builders (Toys to Grow On) have soft poly bristles that interlock when pushed together (and stay together until pulled apart). Made of plastic, the pieces come in lots of shapes, including wheel units, half-domes, and pyramids.

Bright Builders (Discovery Toys) come in packets with twenty-four pieces, each a ring with six "satellite balls" that can be combined in all sorts of ways. The units are in six neon-bright colors.

Construx (Fisher-Price) features hollow plastic rods that fit into connector pieces. Add-on and accessory units are available for making a wide variety of structures and vehicles, including glow-in-the-dark pieces.

Playplax (Galt) is a set of interlocking plastic components in six translucent colors. **Octons** (Galt) are similar translucent plastic shapes that are compatible with **Flexi Octons** (flexible opaque polypropylene pieces). **Loctagons** (Lauri) are a similar product.

Wooden Sets

Tinkertoy (Playskool) is still highly popular with children beginning at age three. The sets feature wooden building poles and dowels but have plastic wheels. Children enjoy making stick creatures, vehicles, and buildings. The **Giant Tinkertoy Building Set** (Playskool) operates on the same principle as the standard-sized units, except these Tinkertoy pieces are sixteen times their size! The set can be used to create a pirate ship, a five-foot-tall robot, and child-powered vehicles.

First Construction Set (Galt) is similar in building concept to Tinkertoy. This set has fifty dowels, cubes, wheels, cylinders, and rectangular blocks crafted from unpainted hardwood, especially for the three- to six-year-old set.

Lincoln Logs (Playskool) are a traditional wooden building component set. Children enjoy building log cabins and forts. The "logs" are brown-stained wood building units with an interlocking design. Roof slats, gables, and other accessories are included. Lincoln Logs require a more systematic approach to building than Legos or Tinkertoys because the units fit together in a just-so manner.

See also chapter 3, "Blocks."

Words of Caution

1. Keep small pieces away from young children, who may choke on them.

2. Keep sets that include batteries away from children five years and under; batteries pose a potential toxicity and ingestion hazard for them.

20 ◆ Seasonal Toys

Every season has its own specialty items. Consider some of these all-time favorites.

In Winter Sleds and Ice Skates are for children of all ages.

Sno-Tube (Childcraft) is a thirty-six-inch diameter twenty-gauge vinyl tube with side handles. It is sturdy enough to support any family member and is recommended for children four years and older.

Fill the eight-by-ten-foot inner tube with water on a freezing night and by morning, young skaters can be doing figure eights in their own backyard on this **First Skating Rink** (Childcraft). In the summer, the skating rink can be used as a wading pool. It is ideal for the toddler—two years and older.

Safety Skates (Childcraft) are especially for the beginner. They have double runners for extra stability and support, and adjustable straps that hold feet securely. The skates can be adjusted for children about four to eight in age.

Sno-Mobile (Childcraft) is an updated version of a sled. This realistically designed unit allows a child to turn the handlebars to change the angle of the skis for excellent control. The unit, made of rugged plastic, is for one or two riders.

At Holiday Time Consider purchasing an **Advent Calendar** or a **Hanukkah Calendar.** Help children mark off the days until their favorite holiday!

In Summer **Flippers** and **Snorkels** add to water fun. If you are a pool owner, you might consider purchasing a net for water volleyball games.

Roller Skates (Fisher-Price) are adjustable to fit children's shoe sizes six to twelve. The bright primary color skates have Velcro fasteners on ankle straps. These skates have both toe and heel stops and a wheel-control mechanism that keeps the skates from rolling backward. (The mechanism can be switched off as a child matures.)

Word of Caution Purchase items that are appropriate for your child's age and level of coordination.

21 ♦ Water Squirters

The traditional **Squirt Gun** is popular for water play, but you might want to consider these updated versions, too.

Animal Versions   **Water Squirters** (Childcraft) come in two versions: ostrich and elephant. When a child pulls the trigger on the ostrich, the bird's neck stretches up high; when the child pulls the elephant trigger, the elephant's trunk comes trumpeting down. Both release a fifteen-foot squirt of water. Made of durable plastic, they are for children four years and older.

Jet Versions   **Water Jet** (Galt) has a clear plastic barrel so a child can see the pump action involved. The unit is highly durable and has good "squirt" potential. Childcraft manufactures a similar item called **Plastic Water Pump.**

22 ♦ Picnic Set

Picnics are fun for children of all ages. **Picnic Set** (Fisher-Price) makes a child-sized picnic easy. It encourages children to play together in creating fantasy stories—whether indoors or outdoors.

Benefits Props and toys that encourage imaginative play give a child several benefits:

- A child develops an ability to concentrate on play tasks for longer periods of time, which tends to result in an ability to concentrate on real-life tasks later.
- A child develops an ability to play a number of roles—often within the same general play scenario. Children learn to see the world from different vantage points, widening their tolerance level for behaviors exhibited by others.
- A child develops an ability to make up stories, including conflicts within a plot, and to resolve those conflicts, which results in enhanced problem-solving skills later in life.

As a child plays with a picnic set, ask,

- "Where are you going to have your picnic?"
- "Why did you choose that spot?"
- "Who will be there?"
- "What will you eat?"
- "Will you play games?"
- "Will anything special happen during the picnic?"

An Outing for Two—or More Encourage your child who is playing alone to take dolls and stuffed animals out for a picnic. Or have a picnic with your child in your backyard—just the two of you.

Your child may create a picnic basket using items from a play tea set or kitchen set. Loan your child an old tablecloth or towel, basket, and plastic items from your kitchen.

23 ◆ Garden Tools and Kits

Set aside a patch of dirt for your child to call his own. Let him make mud pies and mud castles. Allow him to "develop" the ground with toy trucks and earth movers. You can even turn the plot of ground into a garden.

Do you live in an apartment? Consider buying a small wading pool to put on your deck or patio. Fill it with dirt or sand as your child's special farm.

Tools **Garden Tools** (Little Tikes) include a child-sized rake, hoe, and shovel in bright primary colors.

Little Tikes also makes a **Garden Cart**—a sturdy child-sized polyethylene plastic wheelbarrow. This bright yellow two-wheeler has a central handle for stability.

As your child gets older, encourage him to grow a garden. Try radishes, carrots, beans, marigolds, or sweet peas. (One row of seeds may be sufficient.)

Gardens teach wonderful lessons about planting, cultivating, weeding, and harvesting; about patience, planning, and continual nurture.

Kits A number of greenhouse kits are available for indoor growing. With **Plantsters** (Toys to Grow On), the child gets a growing pond—with turtle- and frog-shaped "growers" that hold seeds at the right level for germination—and a watering cup, seeds, pots, "magic soil pellets," and signs for labeling plants. An easy-to-follow activity and instruction guide is included. The **Growing Things** (Galt) kit includes four small growing trays, four assorted packets of seeds, and a seed-sowing guide. Both sets allow children to grow real plants. As such, they should not be regarded as toys. Adult supervision is recommended at all stages.

Hydro-Greenhouse (Uncle Milton Industries) is based on hydroponics, the science of growing plants in solutions of water and nutrients. Children use a futuristic greenhouse unit to germinate seeds and grow real plants. The unit is clean and odorless; it requires no electricity.

See also chapter 46, "Hobby and Science Kits," and chapter 52, "Outdoor Playsets."

Word of Caution Keep seeds and real-growing kits out of the reach of children five years and under.

24 ◆ Wind Toys

Children young and old love toys that fly!

Kites Kites aren't what they used to be. Walk into any hobby or toy store and allow yourself to be amazed at the wide variety of kites, including "trick" and multiple-fly kites for the highly skilled.

Two of the best manufacturers are Go Fly a Kite and Hi-Flyer. These lines of kites offer something for every taste, from simple to ornate, in just about every style imaginable. Assembly usually is required.

Children under eight need to be supervised during all stages of kite use—from construction to flying.

Balloons **Windbags** (Synergistics) are a variation on the kite theme. Shaped like giant oblong balloons, the Windbags are eight feet long. Run with an open Windbag, then knot it, and it will stay filled with air. It can be used in all kinds of outdoor play. Tie two Windbags together for more variations. You can also twist them together to make giant balloon toys.

Klutz features a kit of balloons with a booklet

that teaches how to make animal figures and other sculptures out of smaller balloons—the kind often created by clowns or magicians.

Balzac Official Balloon Ball Covers (Milton Bradley) turn ordinary balloons into highly colorful, outrageously designed action balls.

Words of Caution

1. Never use wire or cord with metal fibers or any other metallic item as part of a kite.

2. Always fly kites in open areas and during good (not stormy) weather. Avoid electrical and telephone lines, traffic, tall buildings, crowded areas, airports, and areas where open flames or campfires may be burning.

3. Children must always be supervised around any type of balloon (large or small). Bits of broken balloon are among the most common items that result in choking and suffocation of children. Balloons are *not* safe toys for babies or toddlers.

25 ♦ Frisbees

In the 1870s, a New England baker named William Russell Frisbie offered a line of homemade pies, which he sold in circular tin pans embossed with the name Frisbie. During the mid-1940s, the sailing of these pie pans became a popular diversion among students at Yale University.

Flyin' Saucers Across the United States in California, Walter Frederick Morrison noted America's interest in UFO's, the topic of a number of movies made in the 1950s. Hoping to capitalize on America's fascination with outer space aliens and flying saucers, he created a lightweight metal toy disk that he manufactured through the Wham-O Company and called Flyin' Saucers.

On a promotional tour through the East, Wham-O's president found Yale and Harvard students tossing metal pie tins, calling them Frisbies and the activity Frisbie-ing. He liked the name, and unaware of the linkage to the Frisbie Pie Company, he trademarked the word *Frisbee* in 1959. The metal disks were soon manufactured in plastic . . . and Frisbees have been flying across the United States (and around the world) ever since.

Frisbees are still produced by Wham-O in a wide variety of styles and colors. They still sail through the air at a flick of the wrist.

Golf   **Frisbee Golf** is a pastime adopted by city parks across the nation. A course is outlined, tee-off positions are marked, and the Frisbee "pins" are positioned. The pins are poles that have a circular metal-mesh net around them. Players try to put their Frisbees in the net with as few tosses as possible. The game can be played individually or in groups.

Children four years and over can fly Frisbees for endless hours of fun and healthful development of motor skills, eye-hand coordination, and large muscle coordination.

26 ♦ "Play Business" Items

Children two years and older enjoy playing "store," "business," "bank," or "office." Few props are crucial for these games, and many items can be imagined or created from household goods. Here are a few toys that fit right into the play action.

Cash Registers **Cash Register** (Fisher-Price) is a plastic child-sized cash register that rings a bell when a crank is turned. It has a drawer that pops open, buttons to push, and plastic coins that fit into color-coded slots. (Although designed for two- to six-year-olds, the toy has small parts that may pose a choking hazard; children under five should be supervised during play.) **Solar-Power Cash Register** (Childcraft) has an eight-digit display and seven functions; a register tape can be pulled by hand. Play money is included. **Petit Charge It! Cash Register** (Ohio Art) comes with plastic coins, credit cards, and a cranking unit to print receipts.

Office Supplies **My First Business** (Child-craft) includes a desk organizer that holds all of the necessities (markers, paper clips, tape dispenser, and so forth). It also has a daily planner, an interoffice memo pad, a telephone message pad, a date stamp, stationery, postal supplies, and a money kit with coins, bills, checks, credit cards, money clip, and wallet. To complete the set are signs that say "Office," "Private," and "Will Return" (complete with clock indicator). Most items can be stored in the expanding file folder. The desk organizer can be used as part of a child's real desk set later. **Kid's Business** (Toys to Grow On) is a similar set, with stacking desk trays rather than a desk organizer and a few other variations on the general theme.

Play Money In playing "store"—or even "bank"—a child needs play money. Galt offers **Playmoney-USA** and **Playmoney-UK**—both of which are generous supplies of bills and coins that are realistic in shape, size, and color.

See also chapter 16, "'Play School' Items," for a child-sized typewriter.

Word of Caution Small children should be supervised when the play includes coins or other small items (such as paper clips and rubber bands) that might be inhaled or ingested. These present a potential choking hazard for youngsters.

27 ◆ Modeling Clay

Modeling clay is a childhood standby—especially appropriate for rainy days and times when parents can play along to promote creativity and artistry.

Clay **Always Soft Modeling Clay** (Peter Pan/Harbutt's Plasticine) comes in eight bright colors and is packaged in sets of long strips or short wide cylinders. The material retains its soft texture, regardless of exposure time to air. **Pate a Moder** (Caran d'Ache) is an always-soft modeling clay available in five bright colors with six-inch sticks (one of each color) packaged together. **Pongo Soft Clay** (Adica Pongo) is a similar product.

Modeling Clay (Fimo) hardens when baked in an oven. The clay comes in thirty-four colors with four three-inch sticks in a package. **Always Hardens Modeling Clay** (Colorplast) comes in individually wrapped brightly colored sticks that dry to a hard texture when left in the open air.

Clay Modelling Set (Galt) has three pounds of nylon-reinforced clay that is pliable and nontoxic; it hardens naturally when left to dry. The kit includes a palette with six paints and a brush, a cut-ting knife, assorted craft sticks, a modeling board, and a guide. You can purchase a four-pound block of clay separately from Galt as well as a **Modelling Material Set** (thirty-two sticks of eight assorted colors) and **Modelling Material** sticks (by the color, six sticks to a packet).

Play-Doh This childhood standard by Kenner is second cousin to modeling clay. The nontoxic compound comes in a wide variety of colors, each color in a six-ounce size. It will stay soft indefinitely if kept tightly sealed. Kenner's **Play-Doh: Fun Factory** (also known as Fun Factory Extruder Toy) includes a factory unit that creates shapes from bricks to laces when the Play-Doh is pushed through it. Also included are die strips, two six-ounce cans of Play-Doh, and a trimmer. The **Rainbow Pack** contains eight six-ounce cans of Play-Doh in assorted colors.

Silly Putty When the U.S. War Production Board sought an inexpensive substitute for synthetic rubber in the early stages of World War II, a General Electric Company engineer, James Wright, created this pliant goo that stretched farther than rubber and rebounded 25 percent better than the best rubber ball. Impervious to mold and decay, it could be exposed to a wide range of temperatures without decomposing. It could pull ink from comic books. Yet, with all of these outstanding qualities, no real industrial uses could be found for the stuff.

It was first called nutty putty, and in 1945, General Electric mailed a sample to several of the world's leading engineers, challenging them to devise a practical use for their new substance. No scientist succeeded. But an advertising copywriter, Paul Hodson, who also operated a New Haven toy store, thought it had great toy potential. In 1949, Silly Putty was rolled into one-ounce balls, put into colored plastic eggs, and sold—eventually to the tune of millions of dollars a year.

Plaster   Closely related to clay are plaster molding kits. Galt has a good beginner set with dog and cat latex molds, sufficient molding powder to create two of each animal, a palette with eight paint disks, a brush, and a booklet of instructions. In addition to the beginning **Plaster Moulding** set, you can buy additional **Superfine Moulding Powder** (Galt) and **Creative Plaster Moulding Sets** (Galt)—with molds in either a "Scenes of London" or "Threatened Animals" series. These are definitely for the older child (at least age six).

Words of Caution

1. Although all of the items listed are nontoxic, children should not put art materials in their mouths.

2. As with any electrical appliance, when using an oven to harden clay, children eight years and under should be supervised and older children provided with safety precautions.

28 ◆ Invisible Ink

Children love secrets. Anything that smacks of secret codes or hidden treasures is a delight.

Invisible Writing **"Yes & Know" Invisible Ink Games** (Lee Publications) are books full of invisible writing that is revealed only when drawn over by a Yes & Know pen (included with each book). The books cover a wide range of subjects.

Secret Kit (Galt) has an invisible ink pen, a developing pen, a magnifier/ruler, and a notepad for writing secrets and codes.

Crime Detection **Detectolab** (Childcraft) offers more than eighty crime detection experiments. Children enjoy sending and deciphering codes; collecting and analyzing fingerprints; examining footprints, clothing, soil, and water samples; analyzing clues with chromatography equipment; and re-creating suspect faces. The kit includes test tubes, invisible ink, slides, safety goggles, a small microscope, and more (batteries are required but not included). **Spy-Tech Invisible Detection Kit** (Tyco) lets children decode and encode messages.

Young sleuths might also enjoy a **Fingerprint Kit** (Childcraft).

Coloring Pads   **Magic Pictures Coloring Pads** (Galt) appear to have blank pages. When children rub over a page with the edge of a coin, however, a picture appears that can then be colored in. The pads come in a variety of themes.

These kits are usually enjoyed by children seven years and older.

Word of Caution   Keep invisible ink and batteries away from young children.

29 ♦ Traditional Favorites

Most of these traditional toys and games are excellent for group play or individual play. They develop fine muscle coordination and eye-hand coordination.

Jacks, Yo-Yos, and Marbles The Klutz Company is a leading marketer of traditional game sets. You can usually find these book-and-toy combination sets in fine bookstores and specialty gift shops. They have a **Jacks** set, a **Yo-Yo** set, and a **Marbles** set, among others. The sets come with books of information and suggestions for activities.

Slinky This long coil (James Industries) that can be "taught" to go down stairs can also be manipulated from hand to hand. Like Silly Putty, Slinky was a product of World War II experimentation. A marine engineer, Richard James, was attempting to produce an antivibration device for ship instruments.

Richard and his wife, Betty, started a company in 1946 to market the Slinky as a toy. It is one of the few toys that has gone on a space shuttle flight to test the effects of zero gravity on physical laws governing the mechanism of springs.

Bingo   Bingo is a favorite of children three years and older. **Picture Bingo** (Pressman) has nine illustration bingo cards (with scenes of objects familiar to children) to which playing cards can be matched. **Mr. Mighty Mind** (Leisure Learning Products) matches blocks to perceptual-training cards in a variation on the Bingo theme.

Physical Skill Testers   **Juggling Sets** (many manufacturers) come in a variety of designs. I suggest those made of bean bag components, some of which are available in clever shapes (such as slices of pie, salad vegetables, or segments of a hamburger).

Pick-up-Sticks (many manufacturers) are another favorite of children. **Anna Banana Jump Rope Set** (Toys to Grow On) has a soft fourteen-foot rope that won't hurt children's legs and a book with one hundred jazzy jump rope rhymes.

Skilts (Galt) are a takeoff on the old-fashioned stilts. These are 4 3/4 inches high with tough grip cords.

Words of Caution

1. I do *not* recommend the Hula Hoop. Hula Hoops can cause muscle injuries to young children.

2. Virtually all of the toys in this section are *not* for children under the age of five. Keep them out of reach of infants and toddlers.

30 ♦ Puzzles

How many times can a child work and rework a puzzle? How many hours will a child spend working puzzles? Both questions can be answered with one word: *lots!*

Knobbed Puzzles   **Large Knob Puzzles** (Salco) are wooden puzzles with a large knob on each puzzle piece so that the young child can lift it and replace it. ABC School Supply also offers a large selection.

Readiness Puzzles   **Junior Fit-a-Space** puzzles (Lauri) are made of crepe foam rubber for two- and three-year-olds. The puzzles feature geometric shapes. **Reading Readiness Puzzle** (Lauri) has letters rather than shapes. **Count-My-Fingers** (Lauri) depicts hands, each with a different number of fingers raised.

Place & Trace Puzzles (Discovery) are made of durable plastic. The pieces fit into simple shapes to form complete puzzles but can also be used as cookie cutters, as molding forms for clay, as part of a matching game, or as stand-alone figures.

Floor Puzzles Usually made of heavy-duty cardboard with wipe-clean surfaces, these puzzles are two feet by three feet. They are available through Toys to Grow On, Galt, ABC School Supply, and Childcraft, among other manufacturers and distributors.

Map Puzzles Both World Map and U.S.A. Map puzzles are good for children five years and over. **Magnetic U.S. Map Puzzle** (Childcraft) reveals topography and state capitals when the state shapes (and names) are removed.

Jigsaw Puzzles The finest **Wooden Jigsaw Puzzles,** in my opinion, are those made by Galt. Some have pieces with pegs; virtually all the figures can stand alone for added play value. Numbers, farm animals, and vehicles are just three choices. Galt also has a **See-Inside Jigsaw.** When the pieces are removed, one sees what the "inside" of that piece might look like—for example, the interior of a cupboard, doghouse, or store.

Cube Puzzles **Picture Cube Puzzles** (Galt, among others) are a fun variation on the puzzle theme. Twelve cubes can be put together in a variety of ways to create six different puzzles (depending on which side of the cube face you are working). **Animal Cube Puzzle** (Childcraft) is for toddlers; eight animals are depicted.

Touch Puzzles Tuzzles (Products for People with Vision Problems) are not only for the visually impaired child. These "touch" puzzles are made of foam pieces in geometric shapes that are cloth covered. They're washable, too.

Puzzle Books Numerous sources offer these books on a wide range of topics. Check for age appropriateness. Children can connect dots, unjumble words, work crosswords, thread their way through mazes, and so forth.

Words of Caution

1. Choose the subject matter of puzzles carefully. I do *not* recommend puzzles linked to television programs that feature characters who engage in violent or occult activity.

2. Age appropriateness is critical with puzzles. Find puzzles that will challenge but not overwhelm your child. Your child should be able to work the puzzle to completion with just a little effort. You can tell if a child is too young for a puzzle by her lack of interest in it. If she can't work it, she'll walk away from it. The older child won't start working a puzzle he perceives as being beneath his dignity.

3. Periodically check puzzles that have knobs to make sure they are securely attached.

4. After washing fabric-covered foam puzzles, check all seams to make certain they are still secure.

5. Keep small puzzle pieces away from young children.

31 ♦ Playmats

Children spend a great deal of time on the floor. You can capitalize on that in both fun and educational ways.

Quilts **Play Quilt** (Fisher-Price) gives the infant a soft defined play area with multisensory activities built in. Each of the four large squares at the center of the quilt has something to touch, press, mouth, or look into. The quilt helps a baby gain eye-hand coordination and motivates the little one to begin rocking and creeping motions to reach for or touch the squares.

Mickey Mouse Activity Quilt (Childcraft) is in the shape of Mickey, who holds a mirror in the open palm of one hand and rattle rings in the other. The bow tie and heart (attached with Velcro) make sounds when pushed. A teething ring is attached, too.

Activity Mats **Super-Safe Tumbling Mat** (Toys to Grow On) is a four-by-six-foot durable tumbling mat that has 1 1/2 inches of resilient, shock-absorbent padding for young gymnasts. The colorful, vinyl-covered mat wipes clean easily. It's both flameproof and mildew resistant. Childcraft makes a **Tumbling Mat** in two sizes: four by four feet and four by six feet. These mats have Velcro strips so that they can be joined together.

You may want to consider an activity carpet for your child's room. Toys to Grow On, for example, sells a circular carpet nine feet in diameter that includes numbered stepping stones leading to a central castle and other areas indicative of a lake and river (or roadway); all are surrounded by the letters of the alphabet (both upper and lower case) in shapes representative of words that begin with the letter (for example, *Mm* are within the shape of a white mouse).

Words of Caution

1. Be certain that items attached to activity blankets or quilts for infants are securely fastened.

2. Teach young tumblers how to spot for one another.

32 ◆ Time Tellers, Letters, and Numbers

Children seem to have a built-in fascination with numbers, letters, and clocks—even before they know what they mean.

Tell Time Even in these days of digital clocks and watches, children need to learn to tell time using an analog clock. **My First Clock** (Childcraft) is an excellent time-telling tool. The central part of the clock's face has a see-through panel that allows children to watch the gears move—this clock actually keeps time.

The traditional nonworking **Clock Face** (Galt) is useful in helping children learn to tell time; the hands on the clock can be moved to various positions. This particular clock face has one-minute divisions.

Simplex Wooden Clock Puzzle (Marlon Creations) is a puzzle in which each pie-shaped piece represents one hour; each piece has an illustration of a bear in an activity common to that time of day.

Teach Me Watch (Playskool) has side-by-side analog and digital faces. **Tic-Tock Answer Clock** (Tomy) is a stand-up owl-shaped clock with an analog face on the bird's front and a corresponding digital display in the owl's eyes.

Learn Alphabet and Numbers **Fun with Letters** (Galt) has illustrated cards and soft, shiny, colorful PVC letters that can be traced to make one's own illustration cards. The set comes with four colored pencils. **Fun to Write** (Galt) is a set of six wipe-clean reusable cards with an easy-to-grip pen that helps children learn to form letters and numbers. **Alphabet and Number Tri-Tiles** (Galt) have illustrated cards that come in three parts. Each "card" is actually a minipuzzle; the only way the card fits together is by correctly matching the letters at the top, the illustration at the center, and the full word name for the illustration below.

Giant Spelling Board (Toys to Grow On) combines a wooden jigsaw puzzle with a spelling board. The twenty-six lift-out letters can be set up in a special groove for spelling.

Number Puzzle (Childcraft) combines time telling with number identification and counting. Each number panel has items in it that reflect the number shown and the time—for example, eight balloons go with eight o'clock.

Magic Math Machine (Childcraft) reinforces multiplication tables. Each equation is on a translucent button that, when pushed, reveals the answer underneath. This toy requires no batteries and has eighty-one equations (from 1×1 to 9×9).

Spelling and Counting Wheel (Pressman) holds letters and numbers in grooves. When an inner wheel is turned to match a letter or number on the outer rim, the letter or number units can be slid into place to form words at the center of the wheel.

Magnetic Capital Letters (Playskool) are three-dimensional letters that can be used with magnetic boards or placed on your family refrigerator to spell out messages and names. **ABC's Blocks** (Mattel) are three-dimensional and stackable.

Alphabet Sponge Painters (Toys to Grow On) can be used in the bathtub or used as stamps to make posters and other free-form designs.

See 'N' Say (Mattel) is a favorite of children two and three years old. A rotating alphabet and number wheel is activated when the child manipulates a lever, which results in a "voice" speaking the letter or number. **Touch and Tell** (Texas Instruments) is a similar device; the child touches an illustrated panel and a voice names the letter, number, object, shape, or animal (batteries are required but not included).

Word of Caution   Keep small items, batteries, cords, and sponge paints away from children five years and under.

33 ◆ Memory and Learning Games

A number of products invite children to develop their memory, math problem-solving, reading, and spelling skills.

Cards **Memory Cards** (Milton Bradley) are a preschool favorite. **The Original Memory Game** features picture cards of apples, pencils, dogs, and other everyday objects. The **Animal Families** cards depict baby animals to be matched with their mother animals; the **Fronts & Backs** cards ask the prereader to match the front and the back of an object.

Flash Cards: ABCs (Milton Bradley) are geared for beginning readers (and prereaders). The oversized cards introduce children to letter sounds, with object pictures accompanying the letters. **Flash Cards: Math** (Milton Bradley) help children learn the basic math skills: addition, subtraction, multiplication, and division.

Bull's Eye flash cards have holes in them. Children put their fingers through the holes of the cards that have the right answer to a question asked by an adult. The set covers long vowel

sounds, short vowel sounds, and beginning conso-
nants.

Electronic Toys The *Consumer Reports* top-
rated electronic toys that teach reading, math, and
spelling skills are the "Speak" series produced by
Texas Instruments. **Speak & Read** helps beginning readers master vocabulary, reading, and language comprehension skills. A voice "talks," guid-
ing the child through games and more than 250
basic words. **Speak & Spell** helps children with
150 words of difficult spelling at four skill levels.
Speak & Math allows children to work 100,000
random and preprogrammed problems in addition,
subtraction, multiplication, and division, as well as
play math games.

Little Professor, also from Texas Instruments,
is a hand-held math learning toy. It has 50,000
programmable problems in addition, subtraction,
multiplication, and division. The toy has an auto-
matic shutoff device for saving power when it isn't
being used.

Words of Caution

1. Because of toxicity and choking hazards, batteries should be kept away from children five years
and under. If electrical adapters are used, children
eight years and under need to be supervised.

2. I do *not* recommend flash cards for children
under the age of three.

34 ♦ Doctor's Kits

Beginning about age three, children frequently express concern and anxiety about their bodies—especially small injuries and visits to a physician. A doctor's kit can help a youngster feel more secure and direct any fears into fascination.

Doctor's Kits **Doctor's Kit** (Berchet) is a good basic kit for preschoolers. So is the one from Fisher-Price.

Obtain **Doctor Costume & Accessories** (Childcraft) and you get a green medical smock, cap, and mask, as well as a plastic doctor's kit that includes a stethoscope, a head mirror, a syringe, a thermometer, a reflex hammer, a badge, a medical chart, a prescription envelope, a patient information card, and two empty bandage boxes.

The Doctor's Office (Toys to Grow On) has a traditionally styled bag with medical instruments and a cardboard medical cabinet filled with supplies. The kit includes toy medical instruments, a twelve-inch skeleton, fake X rays, rubber gloves, a sling, bandages, a fake cast, phony blood, a clipboard, a medical handbook, official-looking forms, signs, and a fake medical certificate for hanging on the wall. You can also get a **Personalized Doctor Outfit** (Toys to Grow On) that has a white lab coat, a working stethoscope, a mirror, and a badge with "Dr." and your child's name on it.

Veterinarian Kits **Veterinarian Set** (Child-craft) comes with a bright red case that can be personalized. In addition to medical supplies, the child gets the plush furry patient of her choice: cat or dog. **Pet Vet** (Toys to Grow On) includes supplies, a scale for weighing patients, a grooming brush, gloves, a stethoscope, and more.

Teaching Tools The lift-up flaps of **Outside-In Book** (Toys to Grow On) reveal the anatomy of various body parts. **Invisible Man** and **Invisible Woman** are plastic see-through models for older children to paint and put together. **Pumping Heart** (Lindberg) is a working model of a heart that allows older children to learn more about the circulatory system.

Words of Caution

1. Keep all small items away from young children, who may ingest them or inhale them.

2. Adult supervision is always recommended when children play "doctor" with one another or when they attempt to treat their live pets.

35 ◆ Puppets

Puppets are every child's favorite storytellers. They help a child improve memory (in learning dialogue) and general language skills. Puppets can encourage shy children to communicate, and they can get children to talk about their feelings.

Finger Puppets The Lillian Vernon catalog features elaborate thimble-style puppets. (These are good travel items!) Lillian Vernon also offers children's gloves with different figures on each finger for instant puppetry.

Theatre Childcraft has a freestanding **Puppet Theatre** unit with blackboard panels for announcing the name and stars of the show and a cafe-rod-style curtain. The unit can be turned around to double as a general store.

Unusual Puppets **Plush Puppets** (Childcraft) may be purchased individually or as a set: tiger, bear, alligator, and monkey. Each is approximately ten inches long, made of soft acrylic plush.

Peek-a-Boo Puppet (Toys to Grow On) is shaped like a big red apple in its "closed" position.

Out pops a hand-propelled worm with puppet-style mouth so that you can manipulate a message. The worm has a built-in squeaker.

Hand Puppets **Kersa Hand Puppets** (Davis-Grabowsky) are hand-painted puppets based on popular characters from children's literature.

Community Puppets (Childcraft) are durable and realistic hand puppets depicting community-service personnel, including doctor, nurse, police officer, shopkeeper, and salesperson.

Mr. Rogers' Handpuppets (Dakin) include Daniel Striped Tiger, Queen Sarah Saturday, King Friday XIII, and Henrietta Pussycat.

Preschool Source offers a large selection of hand and finger puppets, a puppet stand, a puppet theatre screen, and "families" of puppets (Caucasian, African-American, Hispanic, community workers, and fairy tale characters).

Homemade Puppets Puppets can always be crafted from small paper bags (let your children do the drawings!), or you can make puppets by sewing buttons and other appliquéd felt features to a pair of socks. Encourage your children to design their own characters, to give them unique personalities and "voices," and then to make up plays, with child-made sets. (In this age of video recorders, you might want to tape their performance.)

Word of Caution Make sure all parts of a puppet are securely attached, including seams.

36 ◆ Playground Chalk

Playground Chalk (Brynzeel, available through International Playthings) is one of the most versatile playthings.

Drawings Draw on all kinds of surfaces:

- Sidewalks
- Patios
- Apartment balconies

And then wash off your drawings and begin again. This particular brand of chalk comes in pastel colors, is nontoxic, and washes off easily. Best of all, it comes in chunky sticks for maximum line-drawing power.

Playground chalk is essential for playing hopscotch, for designing roadways through which tricycles and other child-propelled vehicles might travel, and for developing slalom-style runways and mazes for bike riding and skateboarding.

Word of Caution Although the chalk may be nontoxic, children should not be allowed to put art materials into their mouths.

37 ◆ Card Games

Perfect for teaching about taking turns, group-style card games are some of the oldest socialization toys on the market. These games develop the concepts of friendly competition and, in some cases, team play. Some games also develop strategy skills.

Team Play **Uno** (International Games) can be played in teams. Players attempt to rid themselves of all the cards in their hands; running scores can be kept. It is for two to ten players, seven years and older.

Strategy **Rook** (Parker Brothers) has twenty variations. The game requires strategy in bidding. It is for one to six players, six years and older.

A set of playing cards is an excellent item to take along on vacation. Cards keep children quiet and busy during long car or airplane trips.

38 ♦ Board Games

Board games—also referred to as parlor games—teach socialization skills of taking turns, friendly competition, the role of luck in game winning, and simple strategy skills.

Just for Fun **Candyland** (Milton Bradley) is for preschoolers and young readers. Players move their gingerbread men markers through Candyland; it is for two to four players.

Chutes and Ladders (Milton Bradley) is a chance game geared for four- to seven-year-olds. The object of the game is to work one's marker to the top of the board, climbing the ladders as quickly as possible without encountering any chutes. It is for two to four players.

Although perhaps not a true board game, Ticktacktoe remains a favorite with children. Galt makes a wooden version (with an illustrated board) called **Noughts and Crosses.**

Test Yourself **Go to the Head of the Class** (Milton Bradley) poses questions in art, history, language, music, and science. Correct answers and the luck of the rolled dice take players on a race to the head of the class. It is for two to six players, eight years and older.

Junior Trivia (Selchow & Righter) is a five- to thirteen-year-old version of Trivial Pursuit that tests knowledge in various areas. The playing board is accompanied by question and answer cards, markers, and die. It is for six or more players. **Tot Trivia** has six hundred questions and answers that explore science, safety, manners, opposites, shapes, nursery rhymes, and more for three- to six-year-olds.

Jeopardy! (Pressman) tests a player's knowledge in various areas. It is for three to five players, ten years and older.

Money, Money, Money!
Monopoly (Parker Brothers) has been the all-time classic board game for more than fifty years. Players must wheel and deal in real estate on the streets of Atlantic City. It is for two or more players, eight years and older. **Children's Monopoly** (Parker Brothers) is a version for the younger set.

Also on a money-making and money-spending theme, **Allowance** (Toys to Grow On) sends players around a board, letting them earn money and spend it. Children learn to use money and to make change.

Strategic Moves **Sorry!** (Parker Brothers) allows players to circle the board with a series of slides and backward and forward moves, but "sorry!" cards send a marker back to the starting point. A combination of luck and strategy, the goal is to get all markers "home" without being wiped from the board. It is for two to four players, six years and older.

Stratego (Milton Bradley) is a military strategy board and tile game. The object is to capture the opponent's flag through clever strategy. It is for two players, ten years and older.

Artistic Skills **Pictionary** (The James Gang) combines art skills and charades. Players make rapid sketches to communicate messages to team members. It is for four or more players, twelve years and older.

Words of Caution

1. Keep small playing pieces, markers, and dice out of the reach of children five years and under.

2. I do *not* recommend the board game of Dungeons and Dragons. This game has been linked to violent and psychotic behaviors.

3. I do *not* recommend Parcheesi, even though it is one of the most famous and most ancient of games, primarily because of its origin. The game was originally played with India's most beautiful young women as markers. The game was a true male chauvinist's delight.

4. I do *not* recommend Ouija boards. The prem-

ise of the "game" is that a player's fingers can guide a message indicator over the board to reveal a series of cryptic answers. In my opinion, this board opens a child up to occult practices that can be highly dangerous for spiritual development.

39 ◆ Mathematical Games and Logic Puzzles

Games and puzzles are an excellent way to help your child develop logic, math, and reasoning skills.

Matching Games Dominoes (many manufacturers) is perhaps the most classic of all number-matching games. This game featuring black tiles with varying numbers of white dots tests a player's numerical skills. It is for two to six (or eight) players, six years and older.

Galt markets two variations on the Dominoes theme. **Picture Dominoes** has twenty-eight large colorful cards. Pictures, rather than numbers of dots, must match. **The Picture-Word Dominoes** set comes with twenty picture cards and twenty word cards; players must match the word card with the related picture card.

Lillian Vernon offers **Nature Dominoes** that match up spiders, fireflies, grasshoppers, butterflies, leafhoppers, ladybugs, bumblebees, and so forth. The nontoxic designs are silk-screened on wooden tiles.

Tease Your Brain! **Rubik's Cube** (Ideal) challenges players, generally eight years and older, to match colors by twisting and turning the cube. **Rubik's Magic** (also known as **Rubik's Magic Puzzle "Link the Rings"**) is a complex puzzle with eight plastic panels that can flip and flop for hours before the printed rings are linked. This one is for children three years and older.

Rubik's XV and **Rubik's Triamid** (Golden Games) are the newest of the Rubik series of perplexing but solvable brainteasers.

Tricky Puzzles   World Wide Games presents a wide variety of metal logic puzzles. Twisted pieces of metal appear to be permanently locked together but can be separated without force or trickery if you can figure out the way to manipulate the pieces. Also consider **12 Tricky Puzzles** (Toys to Grow On). These classic three-dimensional steel puzzles are smaller and come packaged as a set. (A solution book is included.)

Word of Caution   Keep small playing pieces out of the hands of children five years and under.

40 ♦ Word Games

Word games are a great way for your child to improve spelling skills and increase vocabulary—and have fun at the same time.

Spell It! **Scrabble** (Selchow & Righter) calls upon a player's vocabulary, spelling, and spatial skills. The playing board comes with wooden tiles and letter racks. It is for two to four players, eight years and older. Scrabble was created by the same man, Charles Darrow, who created the Monopoly game. He considered the game a takeoff of a crossword puzzle, and the original game was called Criss Cross.

Scrabble Junior (also known as Scrabble for Juniors) is manufactured by Selchow & Righter. This version is for children ages six to ten. Beginning readers use one side of the game board for matching words and pictures. Older children can play the classic game on the other side. It is for two to four players. **Scrabble People** (Selchow & Righter) is a series of structures and people that have slots into which wooden-tile pieces may be inserted. The units can be stacked and arranged in play with transportation systems and toy vehicles. *See chapters 9 and 10.*

From TV   **Password** (Milton Bradley) is based on the television show by the same name. It tests a player's communication and word association skills. It is for three or four players, ten years and older.

Also patterned after a highly successful television show, **Wheel of Fortune** (Pressman) tests a player's word skills, using a spinner, display board, puzzles, play money, and free-spin tokens. This game challenges a young player's spelling skills and perception skills. (The game is actually a take-off of the famous Hangman's word game. **Hangman** [Milton Bradley] is even closer to the original game. Of course, you can suggest that your children play a pencil and paper version of the game.)

Jumbled Letters   **Boggle** (Parker Brothers) gives players a time limit for discovering words hidden in a grid of jumbled letters. Letter cubes are jumbled for each round, with players competing against an hourglass timer. It is for two or more players, eight years and older. **Boggle Junior** (Parker Brothers) is for prereaders. The letters of a simple word under an illustration must be matched with letter tiles.

Word of Caution   Keep small playing pieces and dice out of the reach of children five years and under.

41 ◆ Classic Strategy Games

These games have no element of chance and rely primarily on strategy to outwit an opponent. Each was originally a military strategy game. Children from the age of seven enjoy these games, which develop the ability to concentrate and to think ahead.

Crown the Kings   Checkers (many manufacturers) asks a player to take markers into the opponent's territory and to capture the opponent's markers. This game first began in Egypt about 2000 B.C., when it was known as *alquerque*. Adapted and modified by both Greeks and Romans, the game was reserved for aristocrats for centuries; hence, the appropriate "crowning" of "kings" when a marker reaches the ultimate position in enemy territory.

Play with Marbles   Chinese Checkers (many manufacturers) uses a circular board. Played with marbles, the game calls upon a player's strategic abilities as well as patience. It is for two to four players.

Capture the Royalty Chess (many manufacturers) matches wits and conquest. Pieces of varying ranks and moves are used to "capture" the pieces of the opponent. For years, this game was thought to have been created by a Hindu living in northwest India in the last part of the fifth century. Recent discoveries, however, point toward the origin of the game in an area of the Commonwealth of Independent States (formerly the Soviet Union). The game appeared in Spain in the eleventh century, and the Crusaders took it with them across Europe, where it was a favorite among the upper classes.

Word of Caution Keep these games away from children five years and under since markers and playing pieces may pose a choking hazard.

42 ◆ Carpenter and Mechanic Sets

The desire by most children to play with blocks and construction sets seems to manifest later in life as a desire to build and to use tools. The completion of building projects helps youngsters develop self-esteem and confidence.

"Pretend" Tools   **Master Mechanic** (Kiddicraft) is something of a bridge between an activity center and a multipiece construction toy. It has no detachable parts but does offer elements that the child can manipulate, such as a screwdriver and a crank.

Big Tape (Childcraft) is an oversized tape measure marked for both inches and centimeters. The tape rewinds when a crank is turned.

I Can Fix It Tool Chest (Toys to Grow On) is for children three to eight years old. It has durable plastic tools and a battery-powered drill with jigsaw and bits. Children can hammer in a big plastic nail, screw in a giant bolt, and saw through a plastic "board." The wrench clicks. The storage and carrying case converts to a workbench. (The jigsaw requires two AA batteries, not included in the set.)

Real Tools Real tool building sets aren't recommended for children under eight years old. The older child, however, can manipulate real tools, especially if they are scaled and weighted for youngsters.

Stanley Jr. Tool Collection (Toys to Grow On) is a real set of Stanley tools in a durable plastic carrying case. The set has a saw, hammer, screwdrivers, pliers, nail holder, wrench set, tape measure, socket set, sanding block, and guide.

Young Carpenter's Tool Box (Childcraft) is a durable plastic case filled with professionally crafted tools scaled for young hands: hammer, saw, level, measuring tape, plane, wrench set, socket set, and more.

Billy Builder Tool Set for Carpenters and Mechanics (Natural Science Industries) is a highly compact twenty-four-piece boxed set of tools scaled for a child's use—saw, hammer, pliers, screwdriver, mallet, planer, and clamps, among other items. Included is a manual for woodworking and mechanical projects.

Build-It-Yourself Woodworking Kit (Toys to Grow On) provides a carpenter's box with lightweight hammer, nails, sandpaper, pencil, glue, and ruler. In addition, young builders get smooth pine pieces and a project booklet.

Word of Caution Adult supervision is recommended at all times for children ten years and under. Preteens should be taught safety precautions.

43 ◆ Sewing Crafts

Sewing is a skill that every child needs to acquire, and the various crafts and toys related to sewing provide opportunities for a child to develop eye-hand coordination. Completed projects build self-esteem and confidence.

Lacing and Sewing With **Lacing Shapes** (Lauri), children lace together objects of matching shape, using heavy-duty cord. With **Cotton Reels** (Galt), children connect colorful plastic spools. A child strings together brightly colored **Fun Buttons** (Galt) with a twenty-inch cord—using various patterns for connecting the buttons, which have different hole patterns.

Hot Lace-Ups (Toys to Grow On) require no needles. Simply thread the cord through the holes of prepunched neon-colored vinyl pieces and create a purse that can double as a hip pack, a keychain, a bracelet, a picture frame, a wrist purse, a pencil holder, or a heart-shaped coin purse.

Lacing Tommy (Ambi) is a molded plastic soldier. A child uses a permanently threaded needle to lace the holes in Tommy's jacket.

Sewing Machine (Lillian Vernon) is a working

child-sized sewing machine with an adjustable tension knob, threader, presser foot, light, and foot pedal. It is made of sturdy plastic. The unit runs on two D batteries (not included) or can be worked with a hand crank. Thread, swatches of fabric, and instructions are included. The unit is suggested for children seven years and older.

Tapestry   **Needlepoint Box Assortment** (Fisher-Price) introduces children to the craft of needlepoint with yarn and a large safety needle. The completed pictures become the covers for small boxes.

First Tapestry (Galt) is a kit with five pre-printed tapestry patterns, three pieces of blank canvas, five skeins of colored wool, a blunt-end needle, and instructions for stitches. **Quickpoint** (Childcraft) is a set that has three printed canvases with large holes for easy stitching, three plastic safety needles, yarn, and simple instructions to complete rainbow, heart, and butterfly pieces that can be framed (frames ordered separately).

Weaving   **Mosaic Weaving Loom** (Smoby) has a board similar to a pegboard and plastic pegs around which yarn is wrapped and woven. The finished projects are lifted from the base and can be used to complete other craft items. **Weaving Loom** (Fisher-Price) actually uses a shuttle. This durable plastic loom, for older children, introduces them to the concepts of warp and woof, and a booklet suggests projects from pillows to tote bags. **First Weaving** (Galt) has a set of pegs called a speedloom, a starter selection of yarns, and instructions. **Bead Weaving** (Smoby) combines weaving and beadwork. Children can make belts, headbands, and bracelets in American Indian style configurations.

Knitting   **First Knitting** (Galt) has a circular loom for French knitting, two child-sized knitting needles, an assortment of yarn, and a booklet of instructions.

Beadcraft   **Creative Beadcraft** (Childcraft) has six hundred colorful polished wooden beads in assorted sizes and shapes as well as heavy-duty vinyl thread so that children can mix and match in creating bracelets, necklaces, and other items. **Mosaic Beadcraft** (Childcraft) is a similar set for making craft-style items. Children place colorful beads on plastic pegboards. When Mom "irons" the designs, the beads fuse into permanent creations.

Words of Caution

1. Make certain all needles are blunt-ended or plastic.

2. Keep all sewing items, especially beadcraft items, out of the reach of children five years and under.

44 ♦ Magnets

Playing with magnets is fascinating to children.

Kits **Magnetism** (Galt) is a packet that has a horseshoe magnet with keeper, a sealed container of iron filings, and a storage tray with a built-in ball run and metal ball. **Magnet Building Set** (Galt) provides a building and storage tray with both magnetic and nonmagnetic panels, four round magnets, two plastic encased magnetic blocks, and pieces in assorted sizes, shapes, and dimensions.

Deluxe Magnet Kit (Childcraft) has five magnets and an interesting set of magnetic shapes. **Magnastiks** (Childcraft) is a set with a platform that has four built-in magnets; approximately ninety other pieces are included. **Magnashapes** (Toys to Grow On) is a similar set.

Included in the **Magnetix** (Presto Magix) set are a folding playboard, eighteen oversized magnets, an educational booklet, and a storage tray.

Pictures **Magnetic Designer** (Childcraft) is something of an art tool. By waving a magnetic wand over colorful magnetic disks under a clear plastic window, a child can create pictures and designs. **Magna Doodle/Magnetic Drawing Toy** (Ideal) is a similar drawing unit, allowing a child to move the magnetic drawing pen over disks and write messages, play games, and so forth. The magnetic creations can be "erased" from the screen by the "magic" sliding eraser. **Magnetic Picture Blocks** (Childcraft) have a series of geometric pieces in bright colors that can be secured to a washable coated-steel board.

Marbles   **Magic Magnetic Marbles** (Childcraft) are large marbles magnetized to attach and reattach in dozens of configurations.

Word of Caution   Keep magnets and the small pieces associated with these kits away from children five years and under; they are a potential threat to young children who may inhale or ingest them.

45 ♦ Art Games and Supplies

The world of art supplies and games is a vast one! This chapter highlights only a few of the outstanding products on the market.

Standard Supplies **Crayola Crayons** (Binney & Smith) are a must for every child. In my opinion, crayons provide the most creativity, play value, and educational value you can purchase for the price of any children's toy, activity, or game. Crayons also help a child develop small motor skills. **Supergrip Crayons** for young children have a knoblike section built into each crayon stick, which makes it easier to hold.

Colorforms (Colorforms) is the classic reusable design set. The flat vinyl shapes adhere easily to a vinyl-covered cardboard "slate."

Etch-a-Sketch (Ohio Art) has horizontal and vertical knobs so that children can draw on the screen without pencils, pens, or crayons. **Magic Design Board** (Childcraft) allows children to draw or write with a special plastic pen, then slide the built-in eraser over the pad to start over.

Finger Paint (Binney & Smith) is nontoxic and may be washed off hands with soap and water.

Children as young as three years old enjoy finger painting.

Crayola Art Workshop (Binney & Smith) is a combination art set that includes boxes of standard-size and large fluorescent crayons, colored chalk, watercolors, poster paint, stencils, a pencil sharpener, mixing cups, colored paper, and a built-in crayon stand. Other sets include **Ultimate Artist's Set** (Childcraft) and **Artworks Colorbox** (Toys to Grow On).

An **Easel** and **Paints** are kindergarten mainstays that can provide hours of fun at home, too. Childcraft makes a sturdy **Adjustable Double Chalkboard Easel.** Childcraft also offers sets of **Poster Paint, Plastic Paint Cups, Easel Newsprint Paper, Paintbrushes,** and extra sets of **Easel Clips.** You may want to consider a tabletop easel instead. **Three-Way Tabletop Easel** (Toys to Grow On) has a chalkboard on one side, a write-and-wipe surface on the other for use with chalk, markers, or paints—plus easel clips for displaying finished masterpieces.

Stencil Sets (Galt; Tupperware) and **Creative Templates** (Galt) come in a wide variety of designs, including numbers and letters, farmyard animals, domestic pets, safari animals, outer space, and others. Tupperware has sets of holiday and celebration stencils. **Designer Kit for Vehicles** (Childcraft) comes with a mini drafting board, triangle, mechanical pencil, tracing pad, guide sheets, and ruler. **Mini Fashion Plates** (Childcraft) combine templates to let young designers create new looks with fine-line markers.

Galt has a full line of art supplies that can be ordered individually: **Paintbrushes, Palette, Safety Water Pots** (that don't spill), **Water Pot Stoppers, Paintbrush Packs, Paintsticks, Coloring Pencils, Fluorescent Crayons, Metallic Crayons,** and **Finepoints** (colored fiber-tip pens).

Various sets provide **Rubber Stamps, Stamp Pads,** and **Sponges** (used with stamp pads). Toys to Grow On offers a **Sponge Painting Kit. Stamp-A-Zoo** and **Stamp-A-Farm** (Childcraft) include both realistic and whimsical animal shapes that can then be colored with **Paintbrush Pens** (sold separately).

Words of Caution

1. Although crayons and most other children's paint and art supplies are nontoxic, children should not put art materials into their mouths.

2. Be cautious in your choice of coloring books. Some are related to children's television programs that contain violent or occult material; a coloring book on the same theme only reinforces those messages.

3. When ironing fabric paints, a child should be supervised closely.

46 ◆ Hobby and Science Kits

Hobby and science kits should be chosen based on your child's interest. Encourage your child to follow through on projects to their completion.

Nature **Bug Box** (Galt) is a magnifying box for collecting and studying a single insect. The box comes with a colorfully illustrated booklet and a pad for making notes.

Giant Ant Farm (Uncle Milton Industries) provides an excellent introduction to insect behavior. A similar set is available from Toys to Grow On; this set includes a certificate to get a supply of ants. Both are unbreakable escapeproof units.

Flower Press (Toys to Grow On) comes with a flower press and special pressing paper. Several frames are included for gift-giving purposes.

Exploring Nature (Educational Insights) is a minibiosphere that lets children conduct experiments involving plants, water, and animal life.

Wood Bird Feeder Kit (Fisher-Price) is precut and ready to assemble, with clearly illustrated instructions.

Chemistry   **Introduction to Chemistry** (J. & L. Randall Ltd.) is a chemistry set for young scientists eleven years and older. The set includes goggles, chemicals, lab apparatus, and materials for conducting almost forty safety-tested projects, all accompanied by directions.

Electronics   **Minilabs Electrolab!** (Educational Design) allows a child to build a crystal radio, bell buzzer, or bathtub motorboat while gaining insights into how electrical appliances and machines work. **Electronics in Action** (Childcraft) lets children make a musical instrument or radio. More than twenty-five projects and experiments are possible with this set, which includes a versatile prewired circuit board, a transistor, resistor, diode, and more. **Electronics II** (Natural Science) lets the advanced young scientist build a phonograph, a solar-powered radio, and other working items.

Ecology   **Paper Maker—Recycling Kit** (Galt) is up with today's ecological concerns! This set, for children eight years and older, has all the materials necessary for making paper. Let your children have the fun of making their own paper (for party invitations) and then decorating it.

Weather Forecasting   With **Bushnell Weather Set** (Toys to Grow On), children forecast the weather. Included are a skywatcher's map, erasable pen, wind gauge, barometer, cloud chart, compass, spectrum generator, and a complete guide for plotting forecasts on a world weather map (using stick-on weather symbols).

Geology **Crystal-Growing Kits** (Toys to Grow On) come in both deluxe and introductory models. The easy-to-use kits have guides and premixed chemicals for producing specimens. Also available is a **Grow-A-Geode** kit.

Multiple Sciences **Quadlab Multi-Science Set** (Skilcraft) lets children explore chemistry, biology, and geology. The kit has a generous assortment of lab materials and a manual that invites children to engage in experiments and scientific calculations and observations.

Solar and Wind Power **Suitcase Science Solar Collector** (Discovery World) has a solar collector, heater, and focusing lens in a kit that teaches about solar energy. More than twenty-five experiments are explained in an illustrated booklet. Discovery World also offers **Suitcase Science Cycling Clown** that teaches the effects of wind force and magnetism as sources of energy. Children build an air-driven fan and use it for experiments.

Word of Caution These kits are for older children and preteens. Even so, adult supervision is recommended. Keep all related materials away from children five years and under.

47 ♦ Musical Instruments

Children as young as five years old can learn to play real instruments, especially keyboard and child-sized string instruments. Small motor and basic sound-discrimination skills are enhanced.

Musical "toys" are geared primarily for younger children. With them, you may be able to determine your child's interests and propensity to play a certain instrument. Some toy instruments are highly realistic. For example, **First Guitar** (Childcraft) looks like a real guitar in three-quarters scale with three wire strings and three nylon strings; it has metal keys for tuning.

Bands **Baby's Rhythm Band** (Battat) is a sturdy tabletop unit that allows children to bang, ring, and chime. Included are a small xylophone, bells, a drum, a push-style popper (with colored beads inside), and a small plastic mallet for playing songs.

Busy Band (Playskool) allows a child to play cymbals, tom-tom, snare, xylophone, or cowbell with drumsticks.

Crazy Combo (Fisher-Price) has eleven instrument components that can be combined to create

various wind instruments, each with a unique
sound.

Piano   **Tap-a-Tune Piano** (Little Tikes) is a
desktop keyboard; children can see hammers
pound xylophonelike plates when they push the
brightly colored plastic keyboard keys.

Percussion Instruments   **Pull-A-Tune Xylophone** (Fisher-Price; Little Tikes has a similar
set) is a pull-toy xylophone that can be played with
mallets. **Instrument Bells** (Lilly's Kids) is a unit
with eight metal bells on a rotating plastic wheel.
The bells are struck with a mallet and are color-
coded to a songbook.

Do you have a future drummer in the house?
Hit Stix (Childcraft) has slide controls on four-
teen-inch sticks that allow the child to create forty
different sounds. A clip-on amplifier attaches to the
child's belt. (This toy requires a 9-volt battery, not
included.)

Rhythm Instruments   **Children's Rhythm
Instruments** are produced by a number of manufacturers, notably Hohner and Bambina. Consider
a tambourine, handbells, castanets, wrist bells,
sleigh bell, harmonica, or kazoo. Some Bambina
instruments are shaped like fantasy animals. **Nine-
Piece Rhythm Band** (Toys to Grow On) has a
tambourine, handbell, plastic maracas, pair of
rhythm sticks, guiro tone block, triangle, wrist
bells, handle castanets, and a jingle clog.

Tape Players and Phonographs **Cassette Player Recorder** (Childcraft) is made of bright red plastic and features a sing-along microphone. **Tape Recorder** (Fisher-Price) has both symbols and words on the function keys; it has a hand-held microphone and headphone. An AC jack makes it electricity compatible. (Both units require four C batteries, not included.)

Phonograph (Fisher-Price) is a solid-state unit with a four-inch speaker and child-sized controls. It has a diamond needle and can play either 33 or 45 rpm disks; it operates on normal household current.

Look Hear (Childcraft) has tapes and phonograph disks of commonly heard sounds. Children are asked to match corresponding photographs to the sounds.

Words of Caution

1. Units that require batteries should be kept away from children five years and under.

2. Electrical appliances should not be used by children eight years and under without adult supervision; children over eight years old should be taught safety precautions.

48 ◆ Models

Plastic glue-together models that depict realistic vehicle and airplane designs are recommended.

Model building should involve preliminary help from a parent. Children need to be taught how to read instructions and how to lay out pieces for sequential building.

Planes **Minilabs Sky Full of Planes** (Educational Design) is a kit that has plans and materials for making fourteen different flying machines, including a hang glider, helicopter, skysail, and prop plane. The planes can be painted and are suitable for both indoor and outdoor play. Children can experiment with airfoils, control surfaces, turns, and dives.

Dinosaurs **Prehistoric Museum Dinosaurs** (Small World Toys) are wooden models of dinosaur skeletons. The pieces of laminated wood can be slipped into position without glue or nails. A book about the dinosaur species and its preferred habitat is included with each kit.

Wooden Vehicles Wood Model Kits (Child-craft) come in two sets, each with poster paints and a brush. Set #1 has fifty-nine pieces that make a seaplane, a helicopter, and a biplane. Set #2 has thirty-six pieces that go together to make a race car and a jeep. Sandpaper and glue are included with clearly written instructions.

Steel Systems Erector (Ideal) is a steel girder construction system that has been updated in recent years to allow children to build motorized robots and vehicles. A plastic chassis simplifies and facilitates precise building. (Batteries are required to operate the devices but are not included.)

Robots Robotix (Milton Bradley) lets children snap together interchangeable parts to create remote-control robots. Joints swivel; pincers pick up items; jaws articulate.

See chapter 34 for information about human anatomy model kits.

Words of Caution

1. I do *not* recommend models that depict monsters, fantasy creatures, or characters adapted from children's television programs.

2. Models are for older children. Keep small pieces and batteries away from children five years and under.

49 ♦ Optical Devices

Children six years and older enjoy using binoculars, telescopes, microscopes, and other optical devices.

Binoculars **Personalized Binoculars** (Childcraft) are bright red plastic binoculars with 3X magnification. This unit is safe for children as young as three.

Telescopes **30-Power Telescope** (Tasco) lets children explore the heavens. It is a hand-held model. **Telescope** (Childcraft) gives a 40X view of the skies and has a removable 2X finderscope that can double as a pocket telescope; this unit has a 500 millimeter focal length and comes with a metal tripod. Both units are recommended for children eight years and older.

Microscopes **Little Looker Pocket Microscope** (Tasco; Childcraft) is a pocket-sized instrument with 30X magnification and bright bulb illumination; it comes with a carrying case. (The unit requires two AA batteries.)

5-Way Microscope Workshop (Childcraft) has

a 50X to 900X zoom microscope with a built-in camera to capture images on film, a clever three-way projection system, and a big activity kit. It adapts to accommodate both individual and group viewing. It has three-way turret-mounted objective lenses and two-way illumination. (Two AA batteries are required but not included, and the unit takes 110 cartridge film for its camera.) **Additional Specimen Slides** are available. The **5-in-1 Microscope** (Tasco) operates as a regular microscope but can project an image onto a wall or table for viewing or tracing and can take pictures with 110 film.

Micro Explorer Set (Fisher-Price) is for children five years and older. The kit has a 30X microscope with detachable microviewer, prepared slides, tweezers, guidebook, eye droppers, and a magnifier-top specimen bottle. (Two AA batteries are required but not included.)

Anywhere, Anytime Kids' Microscope (Toys to Grow On) can be used underwater. It has a removable base and take-along holster, making it readily adaptable to outdoor explorations. Easy to focus, this plastic microscope doesn't require slides.

Camera   Children six years and older will enjoy recording favorite scenes, vacation memories, and friends with a **Camera** of their own. Choose a self-focusing camera (many manufacturers) that uses 110 cassette film for fewer failures and maximum reward.

Specialty Items **Optic Wonder** (Toys to Grow On) is a single optical instrument that unfolds and adjusts to become seven different items, including a compass, a two-power magnifier, and binoculars. It fits into a pocket when folded.

Kaleidoscope (Galt) allows children to see interesting, changing patterns of color through a tube-shaped scope.

View Masters (Ideal) look like binoculars but are really viewers for flat three-dimensional transparent disks that tell visual stories when rotated frame by frame in sequence.

Word of Caution These devices should be kept out of the reach of children five years and under. Children six to ten years old should be supervised when using microscopes.

50 ◆ Travel Toys

Many toys and games already recommended in this book are travelworthy—portable, washable, self-contained, easily manipulated in small spaces, and relatively quiet. Those are the foremost characteristics to consider in choosing a toy or game to take along.

Totes **Fun-to-Go Play Center** (Fisher-Price) is a four-sided tote that has eight activities: teethers, squeakers, bells, and balls.

Giggly Wiggly Survival Kit (Toys to Grow On) is a cloth tote with a fold-out picture book and four small babyproof toys that spin, crank, toot, rattle, and shake and are safe to use as teethers.

Learning Curves Fun Tote (Panosh Place) has a removable panel featuring a telephone, book, clock, and hoop with soft balls. A shape sorter, built into the frame of the tote, helps babies learn shapes and colors.

Car Seat Compatible **Li'l Safe Driver Car Seat Toy** (Mattel) is a washable dashboard that can be attached with Velcro strips to a car seat or stroller. It has six play features. The soft foam unit is safe for young children; a number of the elements make sounds.

With **Busy Baby Car Seat Toys** (Toys to Grow On), a child gets a chain of twenty oversized plastic links to which four toys have been attached.

Attach 'n' Go Stroller Play Center and **Attach 'n' Go Driver** (Playskool) are two units that turn a car seat or stroller into an activity center.

Designing Traveler   Travel Spirograph

(Childcraft) comes with fifty sheets of paper, red and blue pens, and six design disks, all of which fit into a compartment in the bottom of the sturdy plastic pocket-sized unit.

Games   Many games for children are available

in travel sizes. **Great Games to Go** (Toys to Grow On) is a set of three sturdy plastic mazes. You can find magnetic and peg sets of **Chess, Checkers, Ticktacktoe,** and **Chinese Checkers. Games to Go** (Childcraft) has three classic games (Tic Tac Toe, Solitair, and Fit-the-Shapes) on five-inch square boards.

The World's Greatest Travel Game (Whitehall) has fifty picture cubes and a total of 250 colorful pictures of items that children are asked to watch for as they travel by bus or car.

Word of Caution   Make certain that small

game pieces (such as those used in magnetic and pegboard travel games) are kept away from children five years and under.

51 ◆ Dress-Ups

Children love to dress up in costumes—for most children, the wackier and more outlandish, the better.

Components **Let's Pretend** (Creative Art Activities) has costume components (ordered separately) for acting out roles in offices, restaurants, and store settings.

RoleOvers (Environments) is a fine dress-up concept. Available in several sets, the garment items are designed to be mixed and matched. The pieces are made of washable no-iron fabric and are worn over regular clothing. Various stars, bars, capes, tunics, and hats have Velcro closers or backs for versatility in design and adaptability in size.

Hats **Action Hats** (Childcraft) allow children to switch roles quickly. This set includes a hardhat; hats for police chief, engineer, fire fighter, and race-car driver; and a biker helmet with detachable goggles. You can also purchase an **Astronaut Helmet** and a **Space Helmet.**

Outfits **Police Officer Outfit** (Childcraft) includes a vest with personalized pocket ID, aviator sunglasses, a police watch, safety flashlight, whistle, play handcuffs and keys, badge, and official wallet.

Personalized Cowboy Gear (Childcraft) includes a fringed vest, chaps, cowboy hat, and personalized belt (each ordered separately). Childcraft also offers **Space** costumes, a child-sized **Bridal** costume, and a **Ballerina** costume, among others. **Fire Fighter Set** (Fisher-Price) has costume props children can use with fire-fighting play.

Accessories   **Razzle Dazzle Glamour Box** (Toys to Grow On) has four wildly colored feather boas, two pairs of lacy gloves, two belts, and two feathery hairbows all in a sturdy hatbox. **Jewelry Boutique** (Toys to Grow On) has more than thirty pieces of play jewelry and a yard-long roll of black felt for displaying it all.

Word of Caution Keep jewelry, belts, and other items that may have small detachable elements (such as hat decorations or hat pins, insecure buttons, and beaded garments) away from children five years and under.

52 ◆ Outdoor Playsets

Here are some recommended playsets for outdoor use. These items are classified as toys rather than athletic equipment.

Volleyball **Junior Volleyball** (Childcraft) is for both indoor and outdoor play; it comes with a foam ball and a sturdy plastic stand that has a plastic net. The height of the net can be adjusted; this set is suitable for children five years and older.

Tennis **Driveway Tennis Set** (Toys to Grow On) turns any driveway, cement patio, or basement into a tennis court. The set comes with two rackets, two balls, heavy-duty posts, and a net.

Golf **Junior Golf Set** (Childcraft) is for children three years and older. The plaid golf bag contains two "woods," three "irons," a putter, two foam golf balls, and three tees. The clubs have metal shafts and plastic grips and are geared for child play. Childcraft also offers a **Mini Golf Course** with two clubs, two plastic balls, nine plastic obstacles, and nine flag units.

Baseball   **Lil' Sport T-Ball Set** (Ohio Art) provides practice holding and swinging a bat with the reward of successfully hitting balls! Children four years and older develop eye-hand and large muscle coordination.

Bowling   **Deluxe Bowling Set** (Childcraft) is a sturdy plastic set that comes with pins, a pair of balls, and a rack that holds everything together for storage. It is good for children three years and older.

Paddle Ball   **Koosh Paddle Balls** (OddzOn) allow children to play an outdoor no-net version of Ping-Pong.

Tunneling   **Heavy Duty Tunnel of Fun** (G. Pierce) is a lightweight portable tube of cloth (with reinforcing rings) that children crawl through.

Riding, Sliding, and Climbing   **Teeter Totter and Slide** (Sun Products) is a one-piece unit of molded red plastic. U-shaped, the unit may be turned one way to make a rocking teeter-totter; flipped over, it becomes a slide.

Tike Treehouse (Little Tikes) is a brightly colored molded plastic "treehouse" with a four-step staircase and gently sloping slide. This prod-

uct was designed especially for safe and independent play by preschoolers. **Playside** (Little Tikes)
is a good first slide for toddlers; the steps are
placed close to one another for independent climbing.

Quadro (Davis-Grabowsky) is a set made of
easy-to-assemble plastic tubing. Connectors and
panels allow adults to configure houselike structures, climbing frames, and slides.

John Deere offers through its catalog play structures noted for dependability and safety. **Gym Set**
has a double rope swing, four-rung climbing net,
trapeze, and a set of hang rings. The set is made of
heart redwood that never needs finishing, with
northern hardwood dowels for ladder rungs and
rails; the rope is marine grade. A **Fiberglass Slide**
(optional) can be attached.

Other high-quality outdoor sets with add-on
components may be ordered through Childlife or
Environments catalogs.

Sandy Play **Turtle Sand Box** (Little Tikes) is
a turtle-shaped plastic unit ideal for two or three
toddlers. The turtle has a removable shell that
keeps the sand free of leaves and other debris
when the unit is not being used.

Words of Caution

1. Make certain that all gym units and swingsets
are firmly anchored and are stable for rough-and-
tumble use.

2. Virtually all athletic equipment and accesso-

ries are designed for children six years and older. Keep small pieces (such as golf tees) and pieces made of foam away from children five years and under.

◆ Addresses of Selected Toy Manufacturers and Distributors

ABC Infant Toys
Small World Toys
P.O. Box 5291
Beverly Hills, CA 90210

ABC School Supply, Inc.
P.O. Box 100019
Duluth, GA 30136-9419

Ambi
Davis-Grabowsky, Inc.
P.O. Box 381594
Miami, FL 33138

Anatex Enterprises
14666 Titus #7
Panorama City, CA 91316

Binney & Smith, Inc.
P.O. Box 431
Easton, PA 18044

Brio Scanditoy Corporation
6555 W. Mill Rd.
Milwaukee, WI 53218

Britain's Petite, Inc.
Caran d'Ache of Switzerland
19 W. Twenty-Fourth St.
New York, NY 10010

Ceiji-Revell
4223 Glencoe Ave.
Venice, CA 90291

Childcraft, Inc.
P.O. Box 3143
Edison, NJ 08818-3143

Childlife
55 Whitney Street
Holliston, MA 01746

Coleco Industries
999 Quaker Lane S.
West Hartford, CT 06110

Colorplast
Small World Toys
P.O. Box 5291
Beverly Hills, CA 90210

Community Playthings
Route 213
Rifton, NY 12471

Constructive Playthings
1227 E. 119th
Grandview, MO 64030

Creative Playthings, Ltd.
33 Loring Dr.
Framingham, MA 01701

R. Dakin & Company
P.O. Box 7746
San Francisco, CA 94120

Discovery Toys, Inc.
2530 Arnold Dr., Suite 400
Martinez, CA 94553

Educational Insights
19560 S. Rancho Way
Dominguez Hills, CA 90220

Environments, Inc.
P.O. Box 1348
Beaufort Industrial Park
Beaufort, SC 29901-1348

Equipment Shop
P.O. Box 33
Bedford, MA 01730

Fisher-Price
Quaker Oats Company
636 Girard Ave.
East Aurora, NY 14052

Galt Toys
James Galt & Co., Inc.
63 North Plains Highway
Wallingford, CT 06492

Go Fly a Kite, Inc.
Route 141, Box AA
East Haddam, CT 06423

Golden Games
590 Young St.
Tonawanda, NY 14150

Gund, Inc.
Runyon Lane
Edison, NJ 08818

Hasbro, Inc.
1027 Newport Ave.
Pawtucket, RI 02861

The Hi-Flier Mfg. Co.
P.O. Box 280
Penrose, CO 81240

Ideal
601 Doremus Ave.
Newark, NJ 07105

International Playthings, Inc.
116 Washington St.
Bloomfield, NJ 07003

John Deere Catalog
1400 Third Ave.
Moline, IL 61265

Johnson & Johnson Baby Products Co.
Child Development Division
Grandview Rd.
Skillman, NJ 08558

Kenner Products
10114 Vine St.
Cincinnati, OH 45202

Lauri
P.O. Box F
Phillips-Avon, ME 04966

Lego Systems, Inc.
555 Taylor Rd.
Enfield, CT 06082

Leisure Learning Products
16 Division St. W.
Greenwich, CT 06830

Lillian Vernon Corporation
Virginia Beach, VA 23479-0002

Little Tikes Company
2180 Barlow Rd.
Hudson, OH 44235

Majorette Toys, Inc.
Americas Gateway
8820 N.W. 24 Park Terr.
Miami, FL 33172

Matchbox Toys
131 W. Commercial Ave.
Moonachie, NJ 07074

Mattel Toys
5150 Rosecrans Ave.
Hawthorne, CA 90250

Milton Bradley
1027 Newport Ave.
Pawtucket, RI 02861

National Association of the Deaf
Publishing Division
814 Thayer Ave.
Silver Springs, MD 20910

Parker Brothers
190 Bridge St.
Salem, MA 01970

Playskool, Inc.
1027 Newport Ave.
Pawtucket, RI 02861

Presto Magix
American Publishing Corp.
125 Walnut St.
Watertown, MA 02172

Right Start Catalog
5334 Sterling Center Dr.
Westlake Village, CA 91361

Selchow & Righter
2215 Union Blvd.
Bay Shore, NY 11706

Skilcraft
Monogram Models, Inc.
8601 Waukegan Rd.
Morton Grove, IL 60053

Solargraphics
P.O. Box 7091
Berkeley, CA 94707

Steiff Stuffed Animals
1107 Broadway
New York, NY 10010

Sun Products
Wellington Leisure Products
P.O. Box 244
Madison, GA 30650

Texas Instruments
P.O. Box 765
Lake Geneva, WI 53147

Today's Kids
Route 10 E.
Booneville, AR 72927

Tomy Corporation
P.O. Box 6252
Carson, CA 90745

Tonka Toys
6000 Clearwater Dr.
Minnetonka, MN 55343

Toys to Grow On
P.O. Box 17
Long Beach, CA 90801

Tyco Industries
200 Fifth Ave.
New York, NY 10010

Uncle Milton Industries
P.O. Box 246
Culver City, CA 90230

Wham-O Company
P.O. Box 4
San Gabriel, CA 92778-0004

Whitehall Games, Inc.
P.O. Box 227
Watertown, MA 02272

World Wide Games
Colchester, CT 06415

**To schedule Phil Phillips for interviews
and speaking engagements, write to:**
Child Affects
P.O. Box 68
Rockwall, TX 75087
Or call: (214) 771-9839 FAX (214) 722-1721